BOTS

· · · AND · · ·

BODS

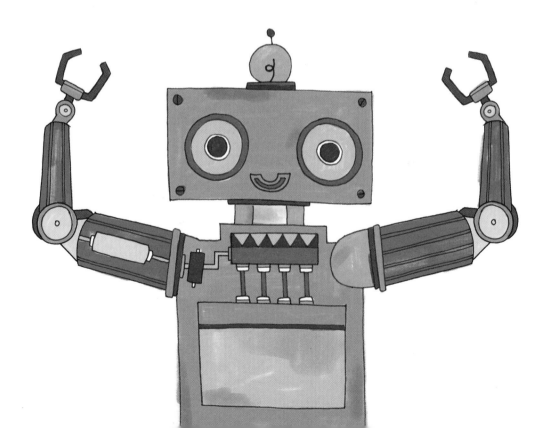

Andrews McMeel Publishing
a division of Andrews McMeel Universal
1130 Walnut Street, Kansas City, Missouri 64106
www.andrewsmcmeel.com

21 22 23 24 25 UNS 10 9 8 7 6 5 4 3 2 1

ISBN 978-1-5248-6275-6

Library of Congress Control Number: 2020947821

Made by:
Sirivatana Interprint Public Co.,Ltd
Address and location of manufacturer:
14/8 Moo 12 Bangna-Trad Road Km 46
Bangpakong, Chachoengsao 24130 Thailand
1st Printing—11/16/20

ATTENTION: SCHOOLS AND BUSINESSES
Andrews McMeel books are available at quantity discounts
with bulk purchase for educational, business or sales promotional use.
For information, please email the Andrews McMeel Publishing Special
Sales Department: specialsales@amuniversal.com

BOTS
·· AND ··
BODS

HOW **ROBOTS** AND **HUMANS** WORK, FROM THE INSIDE OUT

JOHN ANDREWS

Andrews McMeel
PUBLISHING®

Contents

CHAPTER 3: SEEING AND SENSING

CHAPTER 4: THINKING AND FEELING

Introduction

What is a robot? Is it a kind of metal person with flashing lights, making beeping noises and talking in a funny voice? That could be a robot. But it's only part of the story. Some bots look like people, but many don't. They come in all different shapes, colors, and sizes, from the gigantic to the microscopic. Some even look like animals, such as insects, fish, lizards, and dogs.

In 1920, a Czech writer named Karel Čapek first used the word "robot" in a play. In his language, it meant "forced labor." The robots in the play were humanlike machines built to do hard work. In the end, they rebelled against their human masters. Robots started to appear in movies after that, and scientists began to build machines that they called "robots." In the 1960s, the first robots were created to work in factories—and the bot world has been growing ever since.

A robot is basically a machine designed by humans that's programmed to carry out jobs that a person might normally do—or find impossible to do. Robots are built to do things better than humans, and for longer. They make life easier and safer for people by doing dangerous, boring, and dirty tasks. Bots can do exactly the same things day in and day out. They never get tired and always do what they are told. Not many humans can match that!

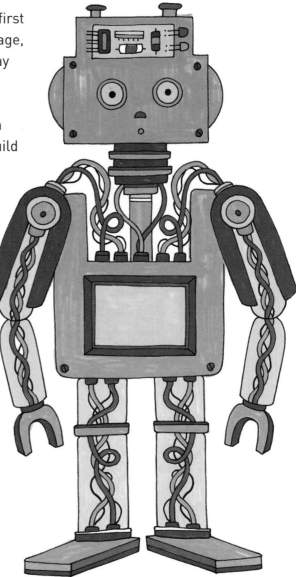

Because robots do lots of jobs that humans might do, they often copy what the human body does. A person needs energy to do anything, from breathing to hitting a home run. A robot needs energy, too, to carry out its tasks. Humans and robots both have to move around to get anything done, and each has different mechanisms for doing that. Anything a person does relies on information gathered by their senses, such as seeing, hearing, and tasting. A bot also has to know what's going on around it and needs sensors to pick up the signals. In a human, all of this is controlled by the amazing brain. Robots have nothing as advanced as that to tell them what to do, but they try their best with the computers and other devices that engineers give them!

In this book, you'll find all the things that humans and robots can do in the same way, and where and how they are different. First, you'll get to know the basic features of human bodies and how they are copied in bots. Then you'll see how movement happens, how the world is seen and sensed, and how humans and robots think it all through. Throughout each chapter are interesting examples that point toward a future when bots will be helping bods more than ever.

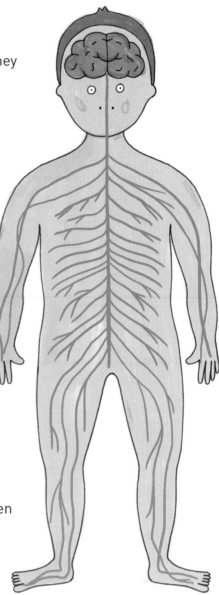

THINK ABOUT THIS...
You'll find Think About This boxes on some of the pages that ask interesting questions about bots and bods. To find the answers, go to pages 90–91.

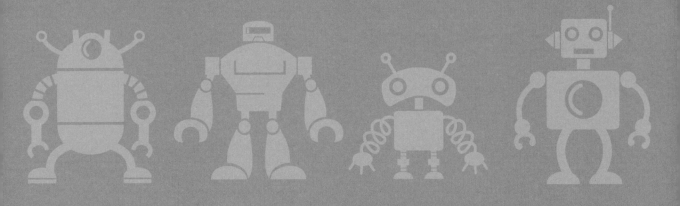

CHAPTER 1:
BODY BASICS

Almost Human

Robots in movies often walk, talk, and even have feelings. In real life, things are different—but bots are getting closer to bods all the time!

A humanoid robot looks quite a lot like a human but also like a machine. It might even say "hello"!

HELLO, I'M A BOT.

NICE TO MEET YOU!

Some robots look a lot like us. They have arms, hands, legs, feet, and heads but are made of metal and plastic. We can still tell they are machines. These bots are called "humanoids." If a robot looks completely human, it's called an "android"—or a "cyborg" if part of its body is human and the rest is a machine. If androids and cyborgs sound a bit scary, don't worry! You'll find them only in sci-fi books or movies!

There are also robots that don't look much like us but that carry out human tasks, like helping people in a hospital, making cars in a factory, or keeping places safe. They can move around, pick up and carry objects, and use tools. These working robots are often quicker at doing what we do, and they make fewer mistakes.

Then there are robots that don't look like us in any way and can do all kinds of things we can't. They can fly, drop into blazing-hot volcanoes, dive to the bottom of oceans, and even explore planets. Some robots look like animals rather than humans and copy what those animals do. There are robot ants, bees, and ladybugs that can fly or crawl into tiny spaces; robot

A drone is a robot that is very different from a human. For a start, it can fly!

FANTASTIC FACT

The first robot that looked like a living thing was not a humanoid—it was a bird! More than two thousand years ago, around 400 BCE, an ancient Greek inventor—Archytas—built a wooden pigeon, powered by jets of compressed air, that could fly. This robo-bird flew about 600 feet before running out of steam. Archytas was really smart. He was a political leader and an expert in math, astronomy, and philosophy.

snakes and lizards that can slither and climb across all kinds of surfaces; robot fish that can swim in the sea—and even a robot kangaroo that can leap a distance of 3 feet! Copying movements like this from nature is a science called "biomimetics." These robot animals may help us go places and do things that would be impossible for people.

We humans are pretty much limited by our size—unlike robots. The tallest human ever was an American man named Robert Wadlow (8 feet 11 inches). The biggest walking robot ever is Tradinno, a fire-breathing dragon (30 feet tall and 51 feet long). Robots can be huge, or they, like a nanobot, can be smaller than this period. There are even invisible robots!

Robots can also figure out how to do things, like pick up a ball, play chess, or cut the grass—but they are always told what to do by humans. Only a human can create a robot. Until a robot can truly think for itself, the most it can be is almost human.

Some robots have human features, like a head and arms, and do human jobs. But they also look really different.

Baby Bods

You were a baby once. Your parents decided they wanted to have you and then made you. Pretty cool, huh? Ever seen a baby bot? Yeah, didn't think so.

One of the most amazing things about humans is that they can make copies of themselves. It's called "reproduction," and all living things can do it. Humans can't do it on their own, though. You need to wait for a woman to release an egg inside her body, and a man to fertilize that egg with sperm, which is made inside his body. If all goes to plan, this becomes an embryo, a tiny human who grows inside the woman in a really stretchy organ called the "uterus." Nine months later, a fully formed baby is ready to leave their mom and enter the world!

But that's only the start of the story. The baby grows into a child just like you, then goes through a lot of body changes as a teenager to then become an adult. When a person begins puberty, they are

I WISH I COULD DO THAT!

ready to begin the reproduction process all over again and help create the next generation of humans. Eventually, we become too old to make babies but can watch our grown-up babies have new babies. It's like a circle that keeps going around and around—the circle of life.

A little more than 250 babies are born every minute around the world—but no robots. Robots can't reproduce, and they have to be made by humans, in factories. Some robots are made to look like a man or a woman, but a bot doesn't need to be male or female. You could make a bot that was the size of a baby, but it would never grow. It would also never grow old, although parts of it would wear out, just like they do on humans. Those bits are a lot easier to fix on a robot. Bots are a lot tougher than the soft, squishy, or easily broken areas of a human.

Robots need humans, though, to make or repair damaged or worn-out parts. In the future, that could be different. There's a machine called a "3D printer" that can make copies of almost any object, including robot parts. These copies have depth, height, and width—those are three dimensions. It's how the printer got its name, and it's how we see the objects around us—their fronts and backs (depth), tops and bottoms (height), and left and right sides (width). If you teach a robot to use a 3D printer, it could make new parts for itself—or maybe even one day create another robot!

THINK ABOUT THIS...

It takes around nine months to make a human baby. This time is called the "gestation period." All animals have different gestation periods. On average, how long do you think it takes these animals to make their babies: red kangaroo, Indian elephant, white-eared opossum, horse, and chimpanzee? And how long does it take to make a robot?

Bony Bits

Humans are soft on the outside, but inside, surrounding all the important squishy stuff, is the skeleton, which is made of strong bones that hold the body together. Robots are pretty much hard all the way through.

You see spooky skeletons every year at Halloween. But they are nothing to be afraid of—we each have one! Your skeleton is strong but light enough to let you move around. An adult skeleton is made up of about 206 bones—long ones, short ones, fat ones, thin ones, and some so small you can hardly see them. Babies start with around three hundred bones, a few of which join together as babies get older. Bones keep you up. If you didn't have them to hold you up, you would just be a puddle on the ground!

The bones inside you are not the dry, hard things you see in a museum. They are alive, growing and changing all the time—so much so, you get a completely new skeleton about every ten years! On the outside of your skeleton is a layer that contains nerves and thin tubes, called "vessels," that carry blood to the bones. The next layer is smooth and really hard—the white part you would consider as being a skeleton—and it contains lots of spongy but tough bone called "cancellous bone." At the center of some larger bones, such as your hip or thigh bones, is a jellylike substance called "bone marrow," and it is where your body makes red blood cells—about two hundred billion of them every day!

TRY THIS...

Want to see how soft a bone can be? Take a clean chicken bone, put it in a jar, and cover it with vinegar. Come back to the jar a few days later, and the bone will be bendy. This happens because the vinegar breaks down a chemical in the bone called "calcium carbonate" and makes the bone softer.

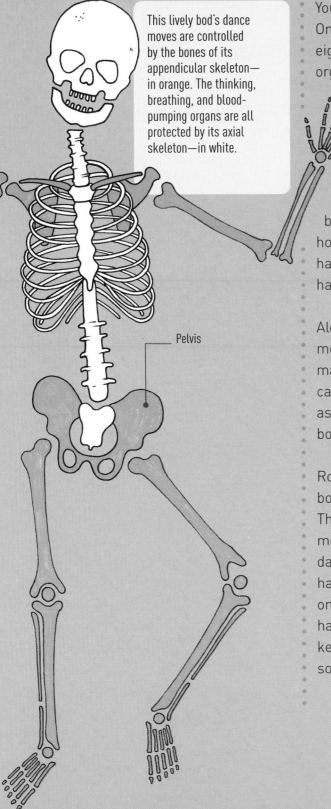

This lively bod's dance moves are controlled by the bones of its appendicular skeleton—in orange. The thinking, breathing, and blood-pumping organs are all protected by its axial skeleton—in white.

Pelvis

Your skeleton is actually two skeletons. One—the axial skeleton—is made up of eighty bones. It protects all the important organs in the center of your body, including the brain, heart, and lungs. The other—the appendicular skeleton—is made up of 126 bones. It helps your arms and legs move. Right in the middle of all of this is the pelvis—a big collection of bones that is joined to your hips and holds up the organs in your belly. Women have a wider pelvis than men because they have to hold a fully grown baby!

Along with holding you up, helping you move, protecting your delicate parts, and making your blood, bones also store calcium, a substance found in foods such as milk and yogurt. Calcium keeps your bones (and teeth!) healthy.

Robots don't need skeletons inside their bodies the same way that humans do. They are held together on the outside with metal or tough plastics, which prevent any damage to the machinery inside. They have something that is more like what is on an insect such as a beetle or ant: a hard shell, known as the exoskeleton, that keeps the insect stable and protects its soft insides.

Outer Layers

What's the biggest organ in your body? Believe it or not, it's the skin. Robots don't have skin—but engineers are working on it!

All animals have skin. The skin of land animals is mostly covered in thick hair or feathers. Reptiles, such as snakes, have tough, scaly skin. Animals that live in water usually have smooth skin, like whales, or scaly but smooth skin, like fish. Humans also have smooth skin, which is unusual for something that lives on land.

There are hairs on your head, of course, but there are also millions of tiny hairs growing out of the skin all over your body. These hairs, and the nails at the ends of your fingers and toes, are made out of a strong substance called "keratin," which also makes bird feathers, fish scales, and animal horns!

Your skin, hairs, and nails are a barrier that keeps the whole body safe. Skin is waterproof; stops germs from getting inside you; and makes sure your body is the right temperature, which is really important on hot or cold days. It has three layers: a thin top layer, called the "epidermis," that is mostly made of dead body cells; the much thicker layer, the dermis, packed with blood vessels and nerves; and a fatty layer, the hypodermis, that holds in heat and energy. The dermis is also full of little pouches, called "follicles," which produce new hairs, and bunches of tubes, called "glands." These tubes push drops of sweat onto the skin's surface to keep it, and you, cool in hot weather. On a cold day, tiny muscles in the skin contract, pulling hairs upright to catch any warmth in the air and pushing the skin upward into little lumps—called goose bumps.

FANTASTIC FACT

Your skin is thinnest on your eyelids and thickest on the soles of your feet. The skin on both of these areas—and your lips and the palms of your hands—has no hair follicles and is called "glabrous skin." Every minute, you lose more than thirty thousand dead cells from your skin—that's around nine pounds a year!

Do robots have skin? Not really—their outsides are smooth and made of hard materials. It's not like the soft stuff that covers our bodies. That means robots are tougher than humans—you can't cut or bruise a robot—but not as flexible. Like us, robots get hot, but instead of sweating, they have fans inside to keep them cool. In really cold weather, robots have to keep moving—just like us!

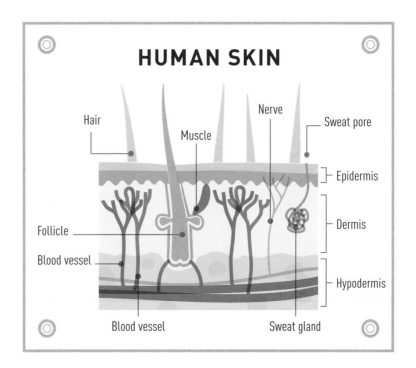

HUMAN SKIN

Hair

Muscle

Nerve

Sweat pore

Epidermis

Dermis

Follicle

Blood vessel

Hypodermis

Blood vessel

Sweat gland

Some scientists, though, are trying out humanlike skin on robots. They call this "sensing skin," because it allows a robot to feel some of the things we feel through our skin. Humans have nerves in their skin to feel things. Robots have devices called "sensors" that pick up information about what is around them. There are even robots that are completely soft! They are made out of a spongy material called "silicone," and they can be any shape, which allows them to squeeze into narrow spaces. Weirdest of all, there are robotics engineers working on robots that can be swallowed! These bots could be useful for looking at our insides.

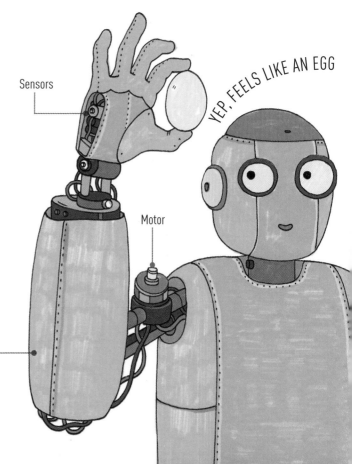

Sensors

YEP, FEELS LIKE AN EGG

Motor

Hard outer layer

Arms and Shoulders

Arms are really useful. They can move in any direction and do lots of different actions like pushing, pulling, and twisting. Robots find arms pretty useful, too.

Your arms' main job is to put your hands someplace where they can do something. This might be holding an ice cream cone, playing with a toy, or even picking up an interesting book about robots! Your arm can do so much because of its three bony joints: the wrist, elbow, and shoulder. A joint is a place where two parts fit together in a way that allows them to move.

There are hundreds of joints in your body, and different joints allow for different movements—up, down, or around, for example. The shoulder is your most flexible joint, and it attaches your arm to the rest of your body. Your upper arm bone, called the humerus, has a ball-shaped end, which fits into a hollow socket in your shoulder, making what is called a "ball-and-socket joint." This means the arm can move in any direction.

Some robots have arms that can do the same job as a human arm. They move their "hands" to wherever they need to be in order to do a particular task. Robots like these are really useful in factories (see

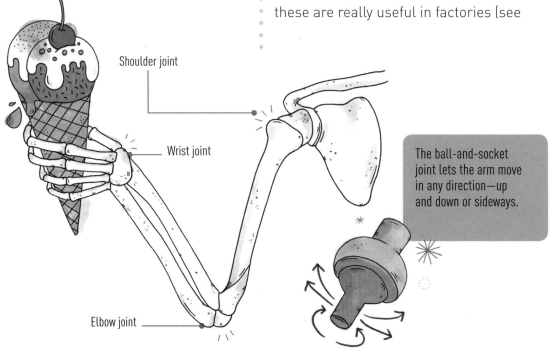

Shoulder joint

Wrist joint

Elbow joint

The ball-and-socket joint lets the arm move in any direction—up and down or sideways.

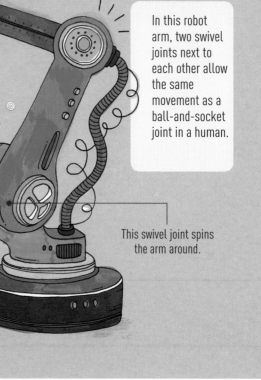

In this robot arm, two swivel joints next to each other allow the same movement as a ball-and-socket joint in a human.

This swivel joint spins the arm around.

pages 22–23), where they can carry out many different actions. The main similarity between a robot arm and a human arm is the joints. Most robot arms don't have ball-and-socket joints. They have "swivel joints," instead. Unlike human joints, these joints can rotate in a full circle, just like a swivel chair. If you put two swivel joints close to each other, you end up with an arm that can move around almost exactly the same as a ball-and-socket joint. This is because one swivel joint can spin the arm around, and the other can swing it up and down.

You might ask why robots don't just have ball-and-socket joints in the first place. It is because two swivel joints are stronger, and they're easier to make and repair than ball-and-socket joints. Human joints are more difficult to repair, although they, including shoulder joints, can be replaced.

THINK ABOUT THIS...

Describing how an object moves can be complicated. There are three kinds of directions: up or down, left or right, and forward or backward. There are also three kinds of rotation: a circular movement, turning inward, and turning outward.

Each movement and rotation is known as "a degree of freedom," and the more of these a robot arm has, the more tasks it can carry out. An industrial robot like the one on this page has six degrees of freedom. Can you find them all? How many degrees of freedom do you think there are in your arm?

Hands and Fingers

There's nothing handier than your hands. And just think of all the hundreds of things you can do with your fingers. It's no wonder that robot engineers try to copy human skills.

Our hands and fingers are amazing. They let you do a lot of the things that make us human—from easy ones like eating, texting, and holding a cup, to harder actions like playing the guitar, making a model, or painting a picture. Along with some other animals, such as gorillas and chimpanzees, humans have thumbs that can be used with the other fingers. These thumbs are called "opposable thumbs," and they allow you to hold and grip objects and tools. It's one of the things that helped human beings become more advanced than other creatures!

Below the skin, hands are made up of three layers: bones, nerves and blood vessels, and muscles and tendons (stretchy, stringy fibers that attach muscles to the bones). There are twenty-seven bones in a hand, which give it structure and allow all kinds of motion in different directions. The muscles provide the power to operate the fingers, which are moved by the tendons inside them (there are no muscles in fingers). The nerves send movement signals to the brain (see pages 54–55), and the blood vessels carry energy to all parts of the hand.

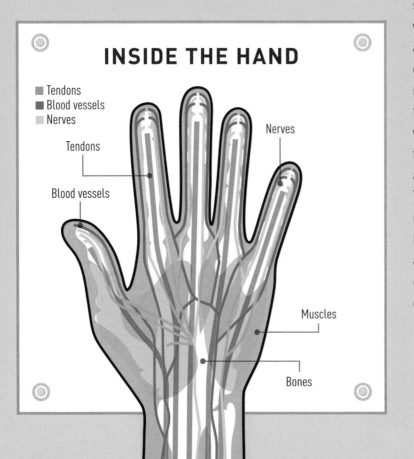

INSIDE THE HAND

■ Tendons
■ Blood vessels
■ Nerves

Tendons

Blood vessels

Nerves

Muscles

Bones

Most robots don't need hands and fingers. They do often simple jobs, like pulling, pushing, or twisting, which they can do using hands that are more like hooks or claws. Some humanoid robots have hands and fingers that look a bit like a human's, with the same kinds of joints and even a kind of opposable thumb.

They can't match the same range of movement as humans have, though, and robot hands and fingers have to be operated using complicated wiring, motors, and computers. However, robot engineers are getting closer to making robot hands that can copy some of the complicated things that humans can do. These hands include devices called "sensors," which can pick up a signal—such as heat, light, or sound—and send that to a computer that will tell the hand how to move. There are even bots smart enough to play the violin, trumpet, drums, and piano!

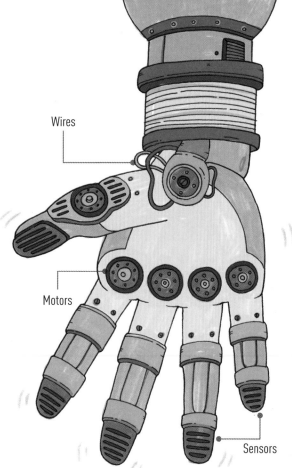

Wires

Motors

Sensors

TRY THIS...

Can you make each of your fingers bend by itself at the big knuckle, without also bending the fingers next to it? Most people find this quite easy for the pointer and middle fingers but not the ring finger or little finger. Why is that? Each finger is controlled by a tendon, and those tendons are all linked. The tendons in the ring and little fingers are more closely linked, so bending one finger can pull the other finger with it! Keep practicing bending all your fingers—it'll come in handy for playing musical instruments or putting on a puppet show!

Robots Making Things

Robots have made a big difference in factories, especially when making complicated things like cars.

A modern car factory might have a thousand robots but only a hundred humans. Some of those people are there to only fix the robots!

Cars are made from metal panels pressed into shape by robots. The parts then go to a kind of moving conveyor belt called an "assembly line," where different robots do different jobs, such as welding, spray-painting, or putting in the engines. Once a robot has finished doing what it needs to do, the car moves along the line, and the next robot takes over. Some of these jobs are done by humans with robot help.

At the end of their workday, the people go home, but the robots keep working. One of the advantages of robots is that they can work all day, every day, and don't need vacations or time off on the weekends. The robots do need regular care so they don't break down, and this is mostly done by humans.

Because robots can work nonstop, using them means that cars can be made quickly and at lower costs because you don't have to pay a robot to work! And since robots will always do the job exactly the same every time, the quality of the cars they make can be very high.

You could even say that the whole factory is really one big and very complicated robot, with some humans inside it!

FANTASTIC FACT

The robots used in factories are themselves made in factories. And yes, they are made by robots. Robots make robots, and the robots you find in the stores might even be robots made by robots made by robots!

Welding robots join together the metal panels.

Automatic painting robots make sure the paint covers all the right parts and is the correct thickness.

People and machines work side by side to put cars together, but the final inspection is usually done by a human.

Other robots add the engine, doors, windows, and other parts.

Legs and Feet

You wouldn't be able to stand up or move around without legs and feet. You have two of each—but robots can have two, four, or more!

Once upon a time, millions of years ago, our ancestors didn't stand, walk, or run on two legs. They found moving around much easier using all four of their limbs. However, early humans realized they had to move fast to hunt animals and reach high places in trees to find food, and they began to stand upright, putting all their weight on two legs. That meant those two legs had to be really strong—strong enough to carry the rest of the body. The legs are made up of the body's longest bones (the femur in the upper leg, and the tibia in the lower leg), the biggest joints (the knee and the hip), and the thickest nerve (the sciatic nerve, which runs from the bottom of your back to your feet). Each foot contains twenty-six bones that have to hold the weight of your body. The wide shape of the foot acts like a platform, from where you can spring up into a run or jump. As you run and jump, your feet soak up the pressure put on the body.

THINK ABOUT THIS...

The strongest tendon in your foot is called the "Achilles tendon." Where do you think that tendon is, and why does it have to be so strong? And where do you think the name "Achilles" comes from?

The hip joint allows a range of leg movement.

The knee joint allows the leg to bend.

The femur (upper) and tibia (lower) are the strongest bones in the body.

Like the bones in your arms and hands, the bones in your legs and feet are held together and moved around by tendons, with the strength provided by powerful muscles, which are given energy from a network of blood vessels. The muscles, bones, and joints in your hips and thighs provide the central, or core, strength in your body. The hip joints are really flexible and allow your legs to move sideways and up and down, and also to rotate inward and outward. Hip joints are ball-and-socket joints, like the ones in the shoulders (see pages 18–19). Each hip joint has to be strong enough to carry your body weight on one leg—like when you kick a ball. You probably know how hard that is from trying to stand on one leg without falling over!

Some humanoid robots can stand on two legs and feet; wires, springs, motors, plastics, and metals take the place of bones, muscles, and tendons. A large motor in a robotic hip gives power to mechanical devices called "actuators," which provide the force to move a robot's legs and feet. However, robots don't have to stand up like we do, and many have at least four legs—like animals rather than humans! They can move around and carry heavy loads much more efficiently and quickly with four limbs.

"Hip" motor powers the robot's legs.

Springs give the legs flexible movement.

Belts or cables hold the parts of the leg together like human tendons.

"Knee" joints allow the legs to bend.

Strong rubber "feet" take the weight of the robot.

Actuators provide power to make movement in the legs.

Head and Neck

Your head is the control center of your body—without it, you just wouldn't work! A robot's controls don't have to be in its head. They could be anywhere.

The essential parts that manage the body and make us feel human are in the head. Biggest and most important is the brain, the organ that tells us what to do and how to think (see pages 72–75). The head also holds the important bits that allow you to see, hear, eat, taste, and speak (all talked about later in the book). The delicate brain, eyes, and other sense organs are kept safe inside a hard, bony mass: the skull. You might think it's just made up of one big piece of bone, but your skull is actually built from twenty-two separate bones: eight form the cranium—mainly the top and back of your skull—and fourteen make up your face. These bones are connected by joints called "sutures," and the only bone that can move is the lower jaw. Your mouth is where air, food, and drinks go in and speech and other noises go out.

Something keeps your head from falling off your body—and that's the neck. Compared with all the things that make up the head, what's in the neck is pretty simple. Don't let that fool you, though—the neck carries two important things that feed your head: messages and blood. Messages travel up to your brain through the spinal cord, a mass of nerve tissues inside the spinal column, which is a long bone that goes from the bottom of your back all the way up to your neck. It is

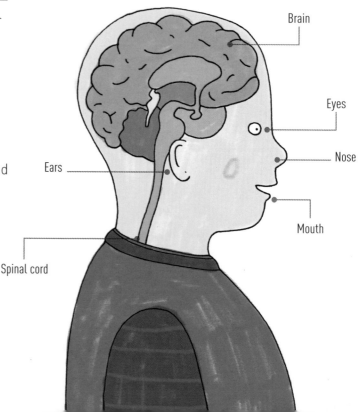

Brain

Eyes

Nose

Ears

Mouth

Spinal cord

made up of thirty-three small bones called "vertebrae." The spinal column enters your head through an opening at the base of your skull. This opening is called the "foramen magnum," which is a fancy Latin way of saying "big hole"! Blood travels into the head through thick tubes called "arteries" and flows away from the head in other tubes called "veins."

Humanoid robots have heads, and sometimes necks, but that's mainly to make them look a bit more like us. A robot's "brain" is its computer, which sends messages to the motors and actuators that make the robot do whatever it has been programmed to do. This robotic control center can be anywhere inside a robot's body, as long as that place is safe and secure, so the computer can't be damaged. When you look at a humanoid robot, its computer could be in its head, or it could even be in its belly!

TRY THIS...

There are lots of muscles covering the bones in your head. These muscles help you smile, blink, eat, and loads of other useful things. How about something less useful? Concentrate hard and try to wiggle your ears. If you can, congratulations! You are one of the 20 percent of humans who can do this, by controlling the auricularis muscles above each ear. All robots could do this—if they were given ears and programmed to wiggle them.

Camera—the "eyes" of the robot

Computer to control the robot

Batteries to power the robot

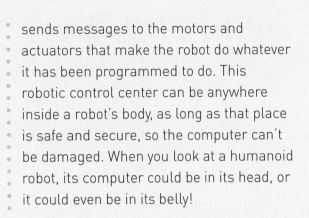

Chest and Back

Your chest is home to the heart and lungs—two powerful organs that keep you alive. Your back keeps your body upright and supported. Robots need support, too, but luckily for them, they can do without complex organs.

Your heart is like an engine in a car, keeping everything moving and working. The heart is basically a really powerful muscle that pumps blood around the whole body by constantly pushing out and squeezing in—between around 60 and 100 times a minute. These are the "beats" you feel if you press a hand against the left side of your chest. Each beat sends blood that is filled with oxygen and other vital substances, known as nutrients, to all the parts of your body—from the top of your head to the tips of your toes. And the heart had started to do this even before you were born!

Most of your chest is filled by two lungs. Their main job is to get oxygen into your blood and remove other gases, particularly carbon dioxide. The oxygen is provided when you take a breath through your mouth or nose, which passes down a pipe—the trachea—into the lungs. There, the breath enters a mass of small tubes, which look like the branches and twigs of a tree. These end in tiny bags, called "alveoli," that push oxygen into the bloodstream and remove carbon dioxide, which you then breathe out. Every minute, you breathe in and out between 18 and 30 times.

FANTASTIC FACT

How long can you hold your breath? The average is between thirty seconds and two minutes, but the world record is twenty-four minutes and three seconds!

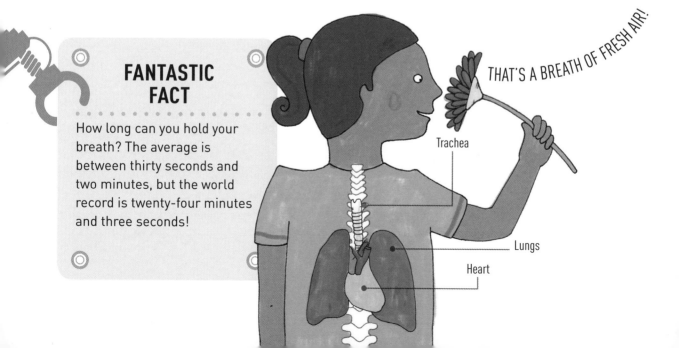

THAT'S A BREATH OF FRESH AIR!

Trachea

Lungs

Heart

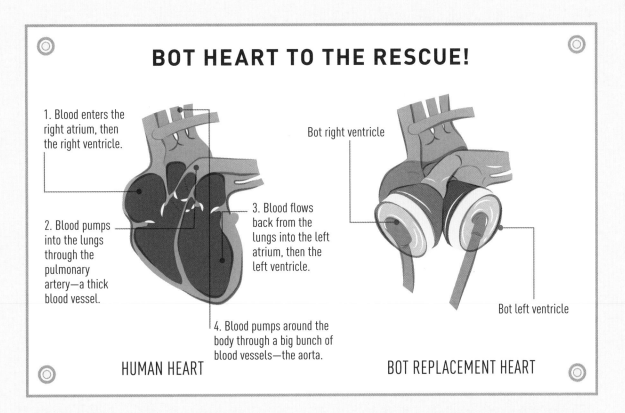

BOT HEART TO THE RESCUE!

1. Blood enters the right atrium, then the right ventricle.

2. Blood pumps into the lungs through the pulmonary artery—a thick blood vessel.

3. Blood flows back from the lungs into the left atrium, then the left ventricle.

4. Blood pumps around the body through a big bunch of blood vessels—the aorta.

HUMAN HEART

Bot right ventricle

Bot left ventricle

BOT REPLACEMENT HEART

Two sets of curved bones—the ribs—plus the backbone and breastbone, protect the heart and lungs. The ribs are flexible, to allow the lungs to expand with each breath. Masses of back muscles provide more protection and support, especially for your spine. They also pull the spine in different directions, which lets you to twist, turn, and bend backward and forward—without falling over!

A robot doesn't need to breathe, but it does need to pump signals and messages through its wires—like blood flowing through the veins and arteries of a human body. This pumping is done by a computer, which is the robot's heart as well as its brain (see pages 26–27). Some scientists have created a way of sending liquid power around the body of a soft robot, a kind of "robot blood" that provides a constant supply of energy to all parts of the body— much like how blood works for humans. It also allows the robot to operate for long periods of time and do all kinds of complicated jobs.

Scientists have also found a way of repairing damaged parts of a human heart with robotic replacements. If the heart's two pumps—the left and right ventricles— fail, two mechanical substitutes can be used to do their same job. One day, there will probably be a complete robotic heart for humans!

Part Bod, Part Bot

Sometimes parts of our body don't work or are lost in an accident. Robots can help by replacing what has been damaged and doing its job.

Amazing though the human body is, it can be easily broken. A person who is badly injured and loses an arm or leg can wear an artificial limb called a "prosthesis." This can help with certain things, but it can't completely copy what a human limb can do since a prosthesis relies on body movements rather than signals from the brain. However, advances in robot engineering now mean that prosthetic limbs not only look like real limbs but also work like them. This kind of science is called "bionics."

Human muscles send out electrical signals that tell the limbs to move. Even when someone loses an arm or leg, those signals are still there in the muscle. Sensors in a robot arm or leg pick up these signals and send them to a computer, which then tells the limb to move. Bionic knees can even detect two types of muscle signals—one for the lifting power to go uphill and one to apply pressure downward when going downhill. Hands are more complicated and need lots of tiny motors in the thumb and fingers to move all the different joints so the robotic hand can grip just like a real hand.

Scientists are also working on bionic limbs that are controlled directly by the brain— just by thinking! Sensors inserted directly into a person's muscle send signals to the brain and then to a computer and motors in the robotic limb. Also, tiny electronic devices that are put into the brain could send movement signals to a mechanical arm, leg, or hand. One day, artificial limbs might even be able to "feel" as well as move, by sending signals back to the brain, which would then react as if the limb were real.

Robots can also help paralyzed people who can't move because they have no feeling in parts of their bodies, especially their legs. These robots, which work like a skeleton on the outside of the body, are called exoskeletons (see pages 14–15). A paralyzed person is strapped into an exoskeleton, which holds the body up, with extra support from a pair of crutches. The person then presses buttons on the crutches to send movement instructions to a computer and motors in the exoskeleton.

FANTASTIC FACT

In 2000, researchers in Cairo, Egypt, discovered a three-thousand-year-old mummy of a noblewoman. To their surprise, on the end of one of her feet was an artificial toe made of wood and leather. This is the oldest prosthesis ever found!

The toe most likely helped the woman walk. Like all ancient Egyptians she probably wore sandals—tricky to walk in with a toe missing. In 2012, researchers in England used a copy of the toe to show that it made walking in a sandal easier!

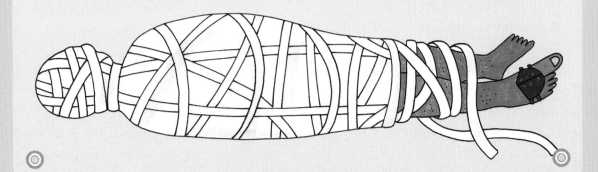

Tiny but Mighty

Some robots are big; some are small. But even the small ones are not always small enough to get into really tight spaces. That's where the tiniest bots come in.

When most people think of robots, it's often the human-sized ones that spring to mind. However, there are tiny bots that can outsmart bigger bots. Some of these mini-robots are so small, a microscope is needed to see them. Others are tiny, but they can join together to make one big robot. Then there are those that can imitate some of the planet's smallest creatures and do similar jobs to them.

Nanobots can repair human cells, like these blood cells. They are injected into the body and move around it through blood vessels.

BOT BODY EXPLORERS

Some scientists have created robots tiny enough to be injected into a human body to carry out repairs or deliver drugs. This sounds more like science fiction than real life! This part of robotics is called "nanorobotics"—"nano" comes from a Greek word that means "dwarf." A sheet of paper is 100,000 nanometers thick, and a nanobot that enters a body is around 50 to 100 nanometers wide. That means a nanobot is a lot thinner than a sheet of paper—that's super small! Some nanobots can help fight cancer by carrying disease-attacking chemicals, known as chemotherapy drugs, through blood vessels to the exact place where the cancer is. Scientists are also working on drug-carrying nanobots with a teeny-tiny lock that can be opened with a signal from the brain. This means a person could control the release of a drug into their body just by thinking!

INSECT POWER

Some tiny robots look just like insects, like ants and ladybugs. Robot engineers study nature for ideas and have copied the motions of insects to create bots that can reach places and carry out tasks that humans can't. Scientists have even created a mini-robot that looks just like a giant cockroach! It's called CRAM, which stands for "compressible robot with articulated mechanisms." That's a complicated way of saying "a robot than can move around and is squashable." CRAM can crawl into small cracks that are half its size. This could help rescuers trying to find people trapped at disaster sites.

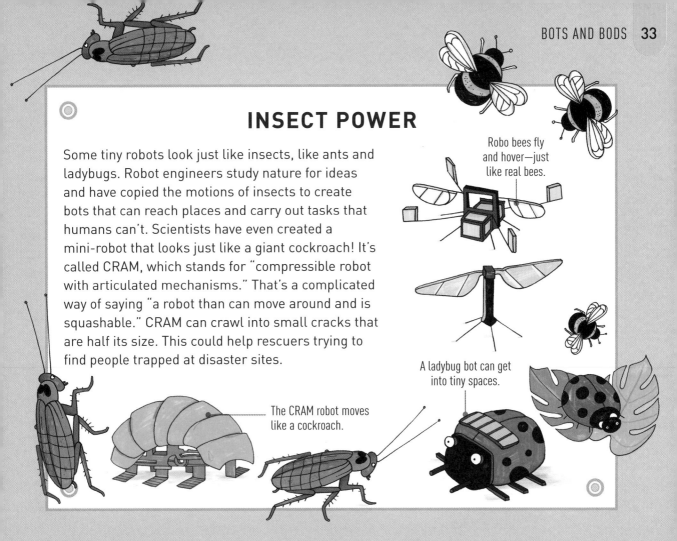

Robo bees fly and hover—just like real bees.

A ladybug bot can get into tiny spaces.

The CRAM robot moves like a cockroach.

POWER IN NUMBERS

Is a robot the size of a small coin going to be any use? Well, certainly, if it's a swarm-bot. A swarm-bot is a miniature robot that can be programmed to join with hundreds of other tiny bots to form a "swarm," like a mass of bees. These swarm-bots "talk" to one another using a kind of invisible light called "infrared." Each swarm-bot is controlled by a tiny computer called a "microprocessor." Swarm-bots move on little wheels or spindly legs and can reach a speed of up to 1 centimeter per second.

Scientists hope that many groups of swarm-bots will carry out useful jobs, such as space exploration and the clearance of dangerously polluted sites.

Swarm-bots are tiny robots, but they can gather together in big numbers—just like ants and other insects—to do exploring and rescue jobs.

CHAPTER 2:
GET MOVING

Muscles and Motors

There are muscles all over the human body, more than six hundred of them. So many are needed because they control every movement a human makes. Robots, however, move by using motors and other mechanical devices.

Whether a person is smiling, lifting a book, walking, dancing—any tiny or big movement of the body—they are using a muscle. People sit on their largest muscle all the time. The muscle in the butt—the gluteus maximus—is important for standing and walking. It's also sometimes called the "main antigravity muscle" because it resists the force of gravity more than all other muscles. The smallest muscle, the stapedius, is only around 1 millimeter long. It's tucked away inside your middle ear (see page 61) and helps reduce noise vibrations.

Muscles only work by contracting, or shrinking, and not by stretching. When the hand is brought to the shoulder, the biceps muscle in the arm shortens. If the hand is brought back down, the biceps relax, and the triceps muscle on the other side shortens. But how do muscles actually work? They are made of bundles of long, thin muscle tissue, called fibers, each thinner than a hair, and each fiber is made of lots of even thinner fibers. One type of fiber is called "actin," and it's like a long rope. Another type is called "myosin," and that does all the real work. It has energy-storing coils and a pair of clamps.

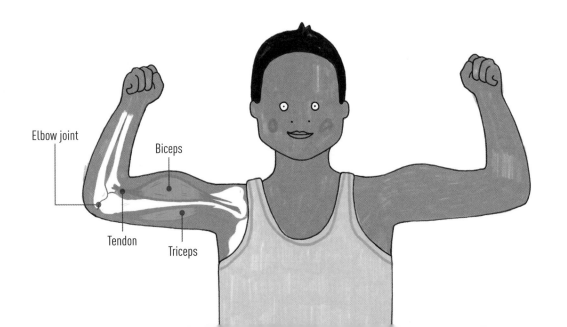

Elbow joint

Biceps

Tendon

Triceps

The clamps grab the actin, and then chemicals in the coils make them tighten up. The myosin pulls the actin toward itself, as if it were climbing a rope. Lots of the fibers do this at the same time, making the muscles get shorter and plumper. That's how arms and legs bend, and why the muscles get harder when they are flexed.

All robots move, but they don't have muscles to help them do this. Instead, they use actuators, which are devices that turn energy into motion. Most actuators are motors, powered by electricity (see page 43), although there are also pneumatic actuators ("pneumatic" means "powered by air") and hydraulic actuators ("hydraulic" means "powered by water"). Different actuators are used depending on the movement the robot makes, such as pushing, pulling, or rotating. A computer inside the robot controls the actuators,

TRY THIS...

With one hand, hold on to a table. With the other hand, feel the muscles in your upper arm. There are two: the biceps on top and the triceps underneath. Try to pull the table toward you, and then push it away. Can you feel the way the muscles get hard and relax, depending on whether you push or pull?

switching them on to make the robot move and off to stop that movement. If a person wants a robot to carry out different actions, all they have to do is reprogram its computer. They can't do that with a human body!

Actuator

Elbow

Computer

Sending Signals

Muscles don't move on their own—they respond to signals sent through the body. Robots also need signals to tell them to move.

When it's time to pick up a pen, turn a page of this book, lift something heavy, or any kind of activity that needs movement, the needed muscle receives a signal to get working. That signal can travel from the brain, through a series of cells called "neurons," to the muscle at a speed of around 270 miles per hour. That's fast! Neurons are also called "nerve cells," and they are part of the body's nervous system, which includes the brain and spine (see pages 26–27)—the central nervous system—and nerves that spread throughout the rest of the body—the peripheral nervous system. The central nervous system controls most of what a body needs to do all or most of the time, such as breathing and blinking, while the peripheral nervous system sends movement messages to muscles.

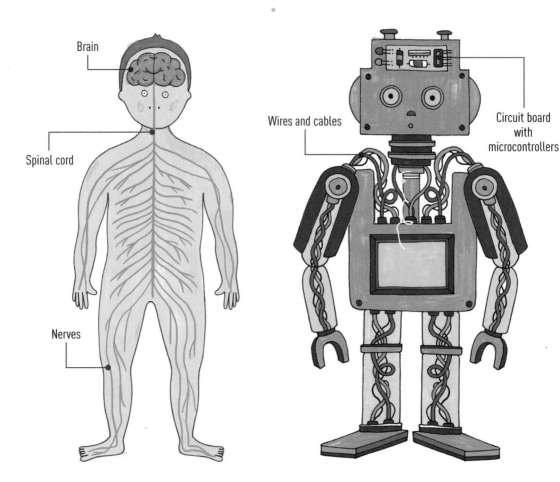

Brain

Spinal cord

Nerves

Wires and cables

Circuit board with microcontrollers

FIRE NEURONS!

The "brain" of a neuron cell is its nucleus. Each cell has lots of fibers that stretch out from its body, including the axon, which is bigger than the rest and sends an electrical signal to the next neuron. The smaller fibers, which look like tree branches, are called "dendrites," and they collect signals from other neurons. Those signals are carried across the microscopic gaps between neurons by neurotransmitter chemicals.

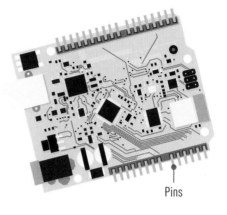

Pins

MICROCONTROLLER

A robot's microcontroller has a series of pins—small, thin metal rods—that can be programmed to send signals to motors that tell the robot how to move.

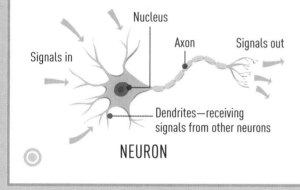

Nucleus

Axon

Signals out

Signals in

Dendrites—receiving signals from other neurons

NEURON

The nervous system contains millions of neurons. The ones that tell muscles to move are called "motor neurons." They send out nerve impulses, which are signals made from electricity. For a signal to happen, a neuron has to get excited! This usually happens when a neuron releases a chemical called a "neurotransmitter," which then causes a reaction in another neuron. The releasing and reacting of a neurotransmitter pushes the signal onward. It passes from one neuron to the next till it reaches a muscle.

A robot doesn't have a nervous system that tells it when and how to move. Its movement signals are controlled by minicomputers called "microprocessors" or "microcontrollers." They are plugged into a central unit called a "circuit board," which also holds other electronic parts, along with the wires and cables that connect to the rest of the robot. Some of these wires tell the robot's motors when to switch on or off, which makes the robot start and stop moving.

Security Bots

Human bodies are pretty strong, but they are easily damaged and need protection from harm. Robots can help in all kinds of smart ways to keep people safe and secure. It's much better if a robot, not a person, gets broken. Sorry, bots!

Because they are made from metals, plastics, rubber, and other tough materials, robots can work in difficult situations where humans might struggle to survive, such as fires, earthquakes, and explosions. Robots never get tired, can stay alert for a long time, be controlled

LIFE-SAVING DRONE Drones can quickly reach places that people can't. They can carry first aid kits, life jackets, and other rescue equipment and get them to people who are in trouble.

BOMB DISPOSAL Bombs cause a lot of destruction, not only in war zones but also in towns and cities. Robots can make bombs and mines safe without any people being hurt.

from a safe distance, and always do what they are told (impossible for most people!). Robots make great security guards. They can keep still and quiet for hours and then warn the police or sound an alarm when something suspicious happens. In the city of Dubai, in the United Arab Emirates, there is even a robot police officer—a "robocop." It has cameras and face-recognition software, so this bot can spot criminals out on the street.

In the armed forces, some robots take the place of soldiers—keeping these military people safe. Robots operated by someone from the army, navy, marine corps, or air force can find mines and bombs and stop them from exploding. Drones—another kind of robot—can fly through dangerous places and gather information. There are also robot tanks and submarines, and doglike bots that carry heavy loads more easily than a soldier can. Scientists are even working on tiny insect bots that are fitted with even tinier cameras and microphones. They could fly almost anywhere and spy on almost anything!

KEEPING WATCH

Patrol robots can wheel silently around parking lots, shopping malls, and other public places, watching for any crimes taking place. The bots can also film what is happening around them.

FIRE FIGHTING
Some fires are too fierce and dangerous for firefighters to tackle. Robot firefighters can get much closer to a fire than a person can because they are made from fireproof materials.

SPIDER BOT When big disasters happen, people sometimes get trapped under fallen buildings. Spider robots can crawl over rubble to see if anyone needs help.

Power and Energy

Humans and robots both need energy to move around and carry out actions. But they are very different in the way they get—and use—their energy.

To get energy, food has to be eaten. When food is swallowed, it travels down the esophagus, a tube about 10 inches (25 cm) long, into your stomach. Inside this stretchy bag, the food is mashed up into a thick liquid, called "chyme," and then flows into the small intestine, where it's fully digested. This mass of tubes isn't "small" at all—it's more than 20 feet (6 m) long in a grown-up! To help break down the food, the pancreas—a spongy, pear-shaped organ—adds special chemicals, called "enzymes," to the mix. All the good stuff—the nutrients—can then enter the blood. The liver, the body's heaviest organ, removes any bad chemicals. Now, nutrient-filled blood can transport energy around the body. This energy keeps people breathing, the blood circulating, the brain working, and the muscles doing what they are told.

How do humans compare to robots? Robots don't need energy for breathing or staying alive, but they need it when they have to actually do something, like moving or lifting.

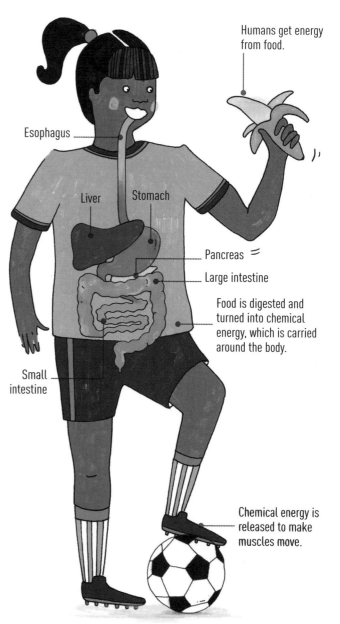

Humans get energy from food.

Esophagus

Liver

Stomach

Pancreas

Large intestine

Food is digested and turned into chemical energy, which is carried around the body.

Small intestine

Chemical energy is released to make muscles move.

ELECTRIC ENERGY

Most robots get their energy from electricity. This is stored in batteries inside the body of the robot. When the batteries run out of energy, they have to be charged with more electricity. Robots use electricity to drive motors to make them move.

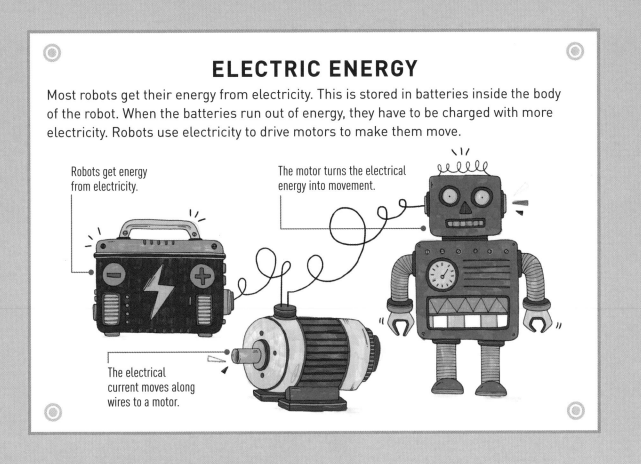

Robots get energy from electricity.

The motor turns the electrical energy into movement.

The electrical current moves along wires to a motor.

Rather than getting it from food, robots get their energy from electricity, stored in batteries inside the robot. Wires from the batteries carry electrical energy to the robot's motors. When the robot needs to do something, its computer tells the batteries to release energy. The computer then tells the motors to move.

TRY THIS...

You can find electricity in some strange places. How about using bananas to charge a cell phone? All you need is a phone, a USB cable, four paper clips, three bananas—and an adult to help. First, bend the paper clips to make them straight wires. Line up the bananas one above the other on a flat surface, with a small gap between each. Join the bananas together by pushing the wires into the left and right sides of the fruit to finish the banana ladder. Push the wider end of the USB cable into the top banana and the other end of the cable into the phone. Wait a few seconds, and you should see the phone begin to charge—banana power!

What a Waste

Once the human body has taken all the energy and nutrients it needs from food, it's time to get rid of the rest—the waste. It's a long process. Robots have it much easier!

When what's left of churned-up food reaches the end of the small intestine, it enters the large intestine—and the final part of the digestion process. The large intestine is much wider than the small intestine, but it's also shorter—about 5 feet (1.5 m) long. At this point, most of the good stuff has been absorbed into the blood, leaving a mix of plant fiber, dead cells, salt, a yellowy greenish liquid called "bile," and water. However, there are still useful nutrients to take out of the food. Millions and millions of tiny organisms, called "bacteria," which live inside the intestines (most bacteria are in the large intestine), feed on the food mixture and help to break it down. Bacteria can cause diseases, but inside guts, they are mostly a good thing!

The walls of the large intestine contain strong muscles, which give it a lumpy look from the outside. These muscles push the food waste along the tube, starting as a liquid and ending as something more solid—your poop! Most of the large intestine's tubing is called the "colon," which is divided into four sections, like

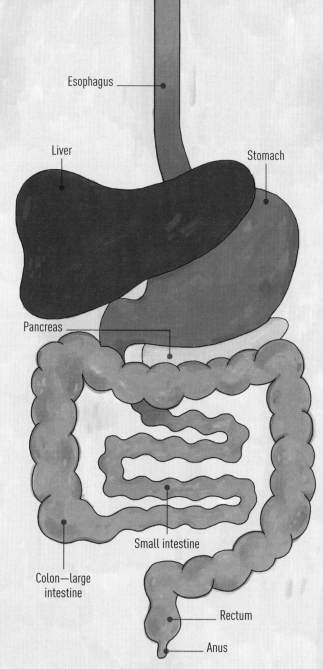

Esophagus

Liver

Stomach

Pancreas

Small intestine

Colon—large intestine

Rectum

Anus

the four sides of a square. The waste (or faeces, as doctors call it) is pushed along the colon until it reaches the rectum, the end of the large intestine. Eventually, your brain tells your anus, at the tip of the rectum, to open—and out comes the poop!

As well as collecting and sending nutrients around your body, blood carries large amounts of liquid. This liquid needs to be cleaned out of the blood and recycled. The blood flows through a pair of fist-sized organs at the bottom of the ribs, on either side of the spine; these organs are called "kidneys." They filter out all the nasty stuff from the blood into a liquid called "urine"—that's pee. The urine passes down small tubes to fill the bladder, where strong muscles hold the liquid in. When those muscles relax, urine travels down another small tube—the urethra—and out the body.

Robots don't eat food or have blood to keep clean, so they have no waste to get rid of. However, they do have to deal with the heat created by their batteries and motors, and the electricity that surges through them. If a bot gets too hot, fans—powered by electricity and controlled by a computer—cool the bot. If this didn't happen, a robot could break down or even start a fire. There are similar cooling fans inside laptops, tablet computers, and game consoles to stop them from overheating.

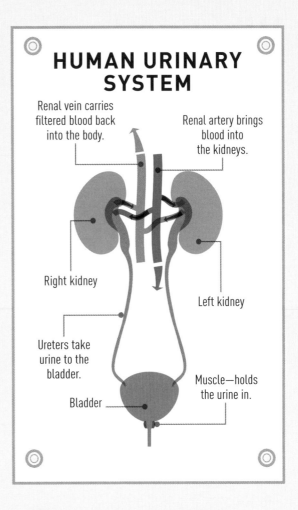

HUMAN URINARY SYSTEM

Renal vein carries filtered blood back into the body.

Renal artery brings blood into the kidneys.

Right kidney

Left kidney

Ureters take urine to the bladder.

Muscle—holds the urine in.

Bladder

FANTASTIC FACTS

The digestive system has around one hundred trillion good and bad bacteria.

Every day, a person's kidneys filter about 48 gallons (182 liters) of liquid from the blood. Around 99 percent of that goes back into the body. The rest—just more than 4 pints (2 liters), or enough to fill about four coffee mugs—is urine.

Walking and Running

You might think it's easy for you to walk and run, but it's hard work for your body. Robots find it even harder.

There are animals, such as apes, that can travel on two legs. However, only humans get from one place to another by walking upright. This puts a lot of strain on your back and legs. Your back has to keep you standing straight and not flopping over, and your legs have to carry the weight of your whole body—and move it forward.

Interlocking bones, called the "spinal column" (see pages 26–27), run up your back and help support your body. Around your spine, a set of dense muscles, called "core muscles," protects these bones and provides the strength for you to stand up straight and move around. When you walk or run, your body pushes down with a big force. This is soaked up by the muscles, joints, and bones in your hips and thighs. The muscles in your legs then push and lift your feet, which act like levers, pressing against the ground to provide the spring you need to walk or run.

No robot engineer can match the complicated mixture of muscles, bones, and tendons that make it possible for you to travel on two legs. Some bots get around on two legs, too, but not as well as humans can. It's not impossible to get a robot to walk, or sometimes even run, like a human—it's just really complicated to put together enough computer parts to get the job done.

THINK ABOUT THIS...

A foal can walk within hours after birth. A puppy is running within four weeks of being born. So why, if people are so smart, does it take a human baby around a year to learn how to walk?

Robots can walk, but they are not very good at running. When humans run, their brain, heart, lungs, bones, muscles, and tendons all work together to create movement, and each leg takes its turn to move the body forward.

BABY STEPS

Newborn human babies take between nine and eighteen months to learn how to walk. As they grow, babies start to build up the muscles that will help them stand and walk.

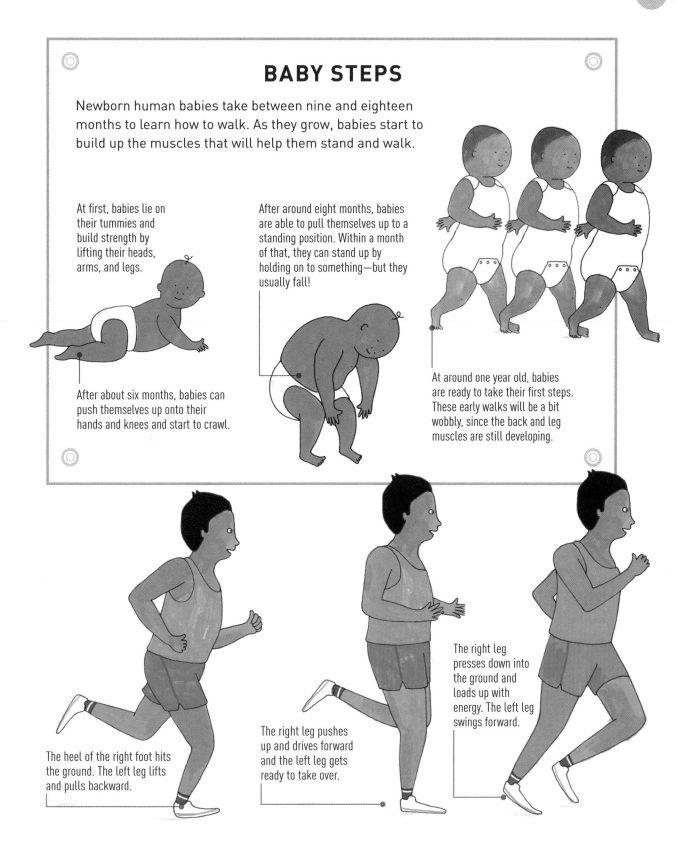

At first, babies lie on their tummies and build strength by lifting their heads, arms, and legs.

After about six months, babies can push themselves up onto their hands and knees and start to crawl.

After around eight months, babies are able to pull themselves up to a standing position. Within a month of that, they can stand up by holding on to something—but they usually fall!

At around one year old, babies are ready to take their first steps. These early walks will be a bit wobbly, since the back and leg muscles are still developing.

The heel of the right foot hits the ground. The left leg lifts and pulls backward.

The right leg pushes up and drives forward and the left leg gets ready to take over.

The right leg presses down into the ground and loads up with energy. The left leg swings forward.

Fastest Bots and Bods

Compared with many animals, humans aren't that quick. It has a lot to do with different kinds of muscles. But don't worry: you can outrun most robots!

You might think you run pretty fast, but you can't run as fast as a cheetah—in fact, no animal can. A cheetah's top speed is around 70 miles per hour (113 kph). The speediest human athletes can sprint 100 meters in less than 10 seconds; the fastest footspeed was 27.8 miles per hour (44.7 kph), recorded by Usain Bolt. Marathoners run more slowly—an average of just 13 miles per hour (21 kph)—but they keep this up for at least two hours. These differences in speed and time have a lot to do with how much muscles twitch! Fast-twitch muscles release energy quickly—good for sprinters. Slow-twitch muscles release energy slowly—perfect for marathon runners.

The secret is the way the muscles use oxygen. Fast-twitch muscles work so quickly, they cannot absorb more oxygen. This is why they get tired. Slow-twitch muscles continually take in new oxygen from the blood, so they get less tired.

How about robots? Can they run as fast as cheetahs or humans? Not yet! For engineers, getting robots to walk on two legs is a big challenge (see pages 46–47). The fastest animals are four-legged, and the same is true of the fastest robots.

The fastest bot

Each of their four legs has two joints (like a knee and a shoulder), which allow bending as well as some sideways movement. This makes it easier for the robot to walk or run over uneven ground.

This kind of robot can run slower than the fastest human sprinters—about 20 miles per hour (32 kph). That's fast for a machine, but not for a dog (and especially not for a cheetah!). Animals have flexible backbones, which allow them to stretch really far to make their strides longer. Robots are usually made to be stiff, since they carry batteries, motors, sensors, and computers.

In this running race, the gazelle takes the lead—but will the cheetah catch it? A long way behind them is the human. Bringing up the rear are the bots. Could they win one day?

THINK ABOUT THIS...

One of the great races in the animal kingdom is between cheetah and gazelle. Cheetahs need to run fast to catch a gazelle, or they stay hungry. Gazelles don't want to be eaten, so they try really hard to escape. Gazelles can run at almost 60 miles per hour (97 kph), which is pretty fast—but not quite as fast as a cheetah. Gazelles' trick to escaping is that they can run fast for longer.

Gazelles are a bit like marathon runners, and cheetahs are like sprinters. What kind of muscles do you think they each have?

Bot Travel

Where's the driver! Well, there isn't one when the robots are in charge. Soon, everyone will be traveling in planes, buses, and trains—and especially automobiles—controlled by bots.

They might not look like robots to you, but self-driving cars are probably the most sophisticated machines you might come across in everyday life. To build a car that can drive itself safely, you need computer-controlled systems and a whole load of computer power. You also need plenty of sensors, which are devices that pick up all kinds of information—such as heat, light, and how close an object is—from their surroundings. The cars have to recognize other vehicles, and people; read highway signs; get passengers to where they want to go; and deal with things like accidents.

Human drivers use their eyes and ears as their main sensors. Both of these are "passive" sensors, meaning they absorb light or sound that happens to be around. Self-driving cars also use passive sensors but rely on "active sensors," too. These send out signals and detect them after they reflect off an object. Three types of active sensor are radar, lidar, and sonar (or ultrasonic). Radar uses radio waves and is used in planes and ships. Lidar uses lasers. Both systems measure the time it takes for a reflection from an object to return to the sensor and works out the direction and distance to that object. Sonar

Self-driving cars are really wheeled robots and have many kinds of sensors.

uses sound waves and is the same technology as the parking sensors used on some cars. It's good for low speeds and short distances.

Robot cars also have cameras that spot highway signs and can tell if a traffic light is green or red. The really smart part is not that the robocars see a sign but that they also read it and make the right decision. Other important sensors include GPS, which shows almost exactly where the car is, and acceleration sensors (accelerometers) that check the movement of a car to detect slippery or bumpy highway surfaces.

BOTS IN TRANSIT

Robot buses have already appeared on the streets in some European cities, such as Helsinki in Finland and Tallinn in Estonia. They work in the same way as self-driving cars but are also controlled from a special center where humans can watch out for any problems. Engineers are also working on railroads controlled by robots and even planes and helicopters that can fly with no pilots. One day, robots will be taking you wherever you want to go!

WHOOPS!

One problem with robocars in the real world is that unexpected things happen. If the car has to make a quick decision, should it save its passengers or any people on the street? And who takes the blame if there's no driver? These are questions that really haven't been solved yet.

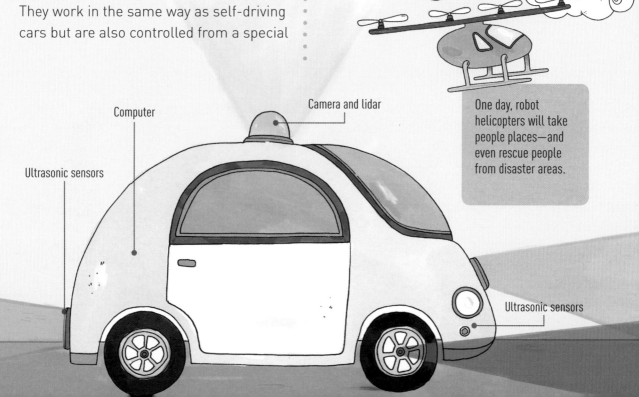

One day, robot helicopters will take people places—and even rescue people from disaster areas.

Computer

Camera and lidar

Ultrasonic sensors

Ultrasonic sensors

CHAPTER 3

SEEING AND SENSING

Fingers and Touch

Where would you be without your fingers? They let you do so many practical things, and by using touch, send vital messages through your body. Robots, too, try to copy these vital senses.

Many of your sense organs are connected to your head—your eyes, ears, nose, and tongue. But some of the most important are in your fingers. These are the main touch sensors, which tell you whether something is rough or smooth, hot or cold, staying still or moving. They do this with a complicated system of nerves, which are a bit like electrical wires. These wires start at your brain and reach every part of your body. They send information back to the brain and also send instructions from the brain that tell the body what to do (like "wiggle your fingers").

Three main nerves in your arm—the ulna, radial, and median—run down its length and into your hand, branching into lots of smaller nerves as they get closer to the fingertips. There are thousands of nerve endings in each fingertip, more than in any other area of skin. These sensors help you feel your way around the world. They let you detect objects as thin as a single strand of hair—0.06 to 0.1 millimeters across—especially when rubbed between two fingers. Each nerve ending has a specialized job, like to detect touch and pressure, feel vibration, or sense hot and cold.

Sensors

Robots rely on electronic sensors to feel what's around them.

There's one more type of nerve—pain receptors. Touch something too hot or cold, or dangerously sharp, and pain receptors send a signal to your brain to pull your hand away quickly. This stops you from accidentally hurting yourself.

Robots are packed with sensors picking up information about a bot's surroundings. However, it's very hard for engineers to make robots that feel the things humans can with their hands. Humanoid robots might be fitted with mechanical hands

TRY THIS...

Get two pencils (not too sharp) and ask a friend to close their eyes. Gently touch one or both pencil tips to your friend's inner wrist and ask if they can tell how many pencils you are using. Try two pencils close together, then farther apart. How many tips does your friend feel? Repeat the experiment, but on their fingers. How many do they feel then? There aren't many sensors in the wrist, so most people can't tell how many points are touching them unless the tips are about 1 inch (2.5 cm) apart. People can detect much closer tips on their fingers.

HAND NERVES

Three big nerves control feelings and movement in your hand. The ulna and median nerves run up the palm of your hand. The radial nerve runs up the back of your hand. They each control different areas of hand sensations.

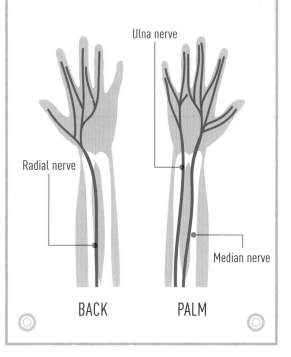

Ulna nerve

Radial nerve

Median nerve

BACK   PALM

and fingers, but they don't have the thousands of nerve endings that you have in yours. Some robot engineers have been able to pack hundreds of sensitive "zones" into the hands and fingertips of androids. This creates a kind of "skin" that can sense tiny differences, almost like a human, in whatever the bot touches.

Eyes and Vision

Suppose there's a carrot on the table in front of you. You know it's there because you can see it. But what actually happens when you see something? And does a robot see the same way?

There are really two different things going on in your eyes. The first is the detection, or seeing, of the object. Some of the light that lands on the carrot is reflected into your eyes, which are light-detecting devices. Your eyes send signals along a nerve to your brain, which conveniently is inside your head.

Then the brain takes over so you can read and understand what you are seeing. It's easy for you to know that the object is a carrot if you already know what a carrot is. Your brain takes all the information it already knows about carrots—their size, shape, color, smell, and so on—and compares it to the object in front of you. The brain does this without you even thinking about it. This is how you can tell that an object is not a banana or a helicopter.

There can be a lot of differences between what you see and what a bot sees. For example, the cameras that work as a robot's "eyes" can see colors

TOO NOISY!

TOO FURRY!

TOO ROUND!

AHA, IT'S A CARROT

FROM LIGHT TO SIGHT

In robots, the process of seeing things is called "machine vision." Electronic cameras are the light-detecting devices, sending signals along wires to a computer processor. This is similar to the way humans see.

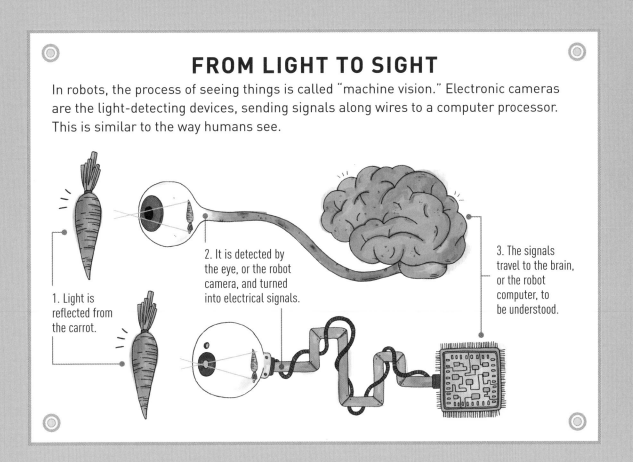

1. Light is reflected from the carrot.

2. It is detected by the eye, or the robot camera, and turned into electrical signals.

3. The signals travel to the brain, or the robot computer, to be understood.

that are invisible to humans, such as those made of ultraviolet or infrared light. A robot camera can also have high magnification, which means it can see tiny things that you can't. Or it might move really fast, so it can see things clearly that are just a blur to you. However, robots are usually not very good at recognizing what they are seeing. That takes a lot of computer power, and usually a robot eye is only trained to see the things it's expected to see. A special carrot-picking robot might not even know what a banana is!

THINK ABOUT THIS...

The tiny pieces of light and color in a photograph taken with a camera are called pixels. A smartphone camera might have ten million pixels (ten megapixels). Do you think the human eye has more or less? If you're feeling really smart, why not take a guess at the number in your own eye.

Robots in the Home

You help out around the house and backyard—of course you do! It's not much fun, is it? Well, there are now robots that can do most of the things people don't want to do!

How cool would it be to have something that could tidy a bedroom, cook a meal, fold clothes, or play games all day—without having to lift a finger? Well, thanks to robots, that's all pretty much possible. One of the biggest advantages of robots is that they can do so many jobs that people find boring, tiring, or time-consuming—and do them without complaining or needing a rest! This is particularly important in factories but is also really useful in the home, where there are many tasks that take up hours that you could be using to do something much more fun.

In the kitchen, robots could soon be cooking whole meals. Engineers have created a bot with two "arms" that are operated by a computer and programmed to make many kinds of dishes. The arms have lots of joints that make them flexible and "hands" full of sensors to recognize all the ingredients and kitchen tools. Plus, a robot will never get a recipe wrong!

Everyone hates cleaning, right? There are robots that can mop and sweep floors, vacuum carpets, and even scrub the toilet. They use sensors to gather information about their surroundings, which an on-board computer processes and uses to make sure the bot doesn't bump into anything—or fall down the stairs! When it runs out of electricity, the bot goes back to its dock and recharges its batteries.

In the backyard, cutting the grass isn't a problem because a wheeled robot is there to keep the lawn looking great—and it only comes out when it's not raining! And why not use a mini-drone to carry small stuff around, and a robot shopping cart to bring home the groceries? With all the chores done, you can now play with your friendly "buddy" humanoid bot.

THINK ABOUT THIS...

Getting up in the morning can be hard. Even if you have an alarm clock, it's so easy just to turn it off and go back to sleep! Now, what if you had a robot alarm clock? How do you think a bot clock would make really sure you got out of bed?

Like all robots, the robot alarm clock is controlled by a computer, has batteries for energy, and motors and actuators for movement.

When the robot alarm clock has woken you up, you can pick your clothes for the day from the laundry-folding robot. It can fold all you need in less than five minutes!

Backyards can take a lot of looking after, especially the grass. Robot lawn mowers make this easy. They have sensors that look out for obstacles, so the bots can mow around them. Some bots can even be programmed to mow in pretty patterns!

"Buddy" robots are great fun for anyone. But they are really helpful for people living on their own, who might be feeling lonely. Some buddies look kind of human; others look like animals—and even have fur!

Delivery robots can bring food right to your door. Like self-driving cars, they use cameras and sensors to understand their surroundings and GPS to figure out where they are going. The customer uses a special code to unlock the bot and get to the goodies.

Vacuum robots mean you don't have to do the boring job of keeping carpets and floors clean. Like the robot lawn mower, a vacuum bot has sensors that show it where to go and where not to go!

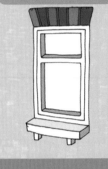

Ears and Hearing

There's much more to hearing than the two flappy parts on the outside of your head. Inside, a lot more ear action is going on. A robot's electronic "ears" are far simpler.

Your ears help you to make sense of the sound vibrations that fill the air. The fleshy, slightly bony part on the side of the head is known as the outer ear. Sound waves enter through the opening you can feel with your finger—the ear canal. The waves then travel through the middle ear and the inner ear to the brain, where the sound messages are all decoded.

The human ear is amazingly powerful; it's able to pick up the tiniest of sounds, like a leaf rustling, or the biggest of noises, like a clap of thunder.

Some animals have even more powerful hearing. Elephants can hear clouds coming, which warn them of storms. Dogs and cats hear really high-frequency noises that humans cannot, which helps them sense when they are in danger.

I'M LISTENING

CAN YOU HEAR ME?

HOW THE EAR WORKS

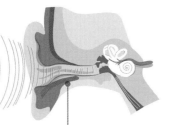

MIDDLE EAR The middle ear contains tiny bones: malleus, incus, and stapes—three of the smallest in the body. They pick up vibrations from the eardrum and pass these through an opening— the oval window—into a snail-like shell, called the "cochlea."

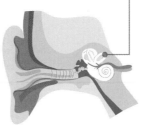

OUTER EAR Sounds enter the ear and move down the ear canal. They hit the eardrum—a little flap of skin stretched tight like the top of a drum—and make the flap vibrate.

INNER EAR The pea-sized cochlea is full of liquid and minuscule hairs. The vibrations from the eardrum bend these hairs, which send nerve signals to the brain. The brain then tells you what you are hearing!

Robots use microphones rather than ears to hear. On a humanoid robot, the microphones might be on its head—but they can be anywhere. They turn sound into a tiny electrical current that travels to the robot's computer, which then "reads" that current using software made to recognize different sounds, including human speech. What humans can hear is limited by the tubes, bones, and other parts inside their heads, but a robot's computer can be programmed to recognize almost any sound, including those a human could never hear. A robot's ability to hear very faint sounds can be useful for rescuing people trapped in remote places or under fallen buildings.

THINK ABOUT THIS...

Loudness can be given a number—a measurement called a "decibel." Normal speaking is around 60 decibels. Sounds that are higher than 85 decibels can hurt your hearing if you're exposed to them for too long. Which of these sounds do you think are the loudest or softest: city traffic, regular rainfall, firecrackers, refrigerator, jet plane taking off, alarm clock, breathing, and hippopotamus? Try putting them in order from softest to loudest.

Keeping Balanced

Ears don't just let people hear things. They also stop them from falling over! It's much more difficult for a robot to keep its balance.

Whenever you move, your ears send messages to the brain, telling it how you are moving and in what direction. All this action takes place in the inner ears; you have one on each side of your head. Inside each, there are three semicircular tubes, called "canals," filled with liquid. At the bottom of each canal is a knob-like area called an "ampulla." Each ampulla contains a kind of jelly, called the "cupula," and a bunch of tiny hairs. The canals detect movement like to and fro, up and down, and rotation and spin. When you move, the cupulae wobble and move the hairs, which shoot signals to the brain so it knows how you are moving.

There are also two little organs, called the "utricle" and "saccule," that detect movements affected by gravity (the force that keeps you to the ground) and acceleration (the action of moving faster), such as riding in an elevator (gravity) or riding a bike (acceleration). Like an ampulla, the utricle and saccule are also filled with a jellylike substance and little

THE BALANCE MACHINE

The body is kept balanced by a smart set of organs deep inside the head that send movement messages to the brain.

hairs that shift with movement and send signals to the brain. The brain then combines these signals with information from the eyes, skin, and muscles to determine where the body is and keep it the right way up!

If you spin around and around, you get dizzy. But how does that happen? When you spin, the liquid inside the inner ear canals moves quicker and quicker, until it's rotating as fast as the spin. Once that happens, the little hairs stop moving, so your brain thinks your body has stopped moving. When your body actually does stop, the liquid keeps on spinning, and the hairs move; your brain tells you that you are still moving—and that's the dizziness. Ballet dancers have to teach their brains not to think they are still moving once they have stopped a spin.

Without brains to tell them what to do, robots have balancing problems. A human can balance fairly easily on one leg, but for a robot, that would take huge amounts of computing power and programming, and loads of sensors to gather data about its surroundings and position. Some robots also use gyroscopes and accelerometers to sense movement and speed. A gyroscope is a spinning wheel held in a frame. It can tell a robot how to correct its movement and keep balanced. An accelerometer is a device that recognizes changes in speed that could affect movement and sends the information to the bot's computer so it can make adjustments. In the end, if you want a bot to balance, put it on wheels, tracks, or more than two legs!

FANTASTIC FACT

You hear music better with your left ear than your right ear. From when you're born, your right ear is highly tuned to speech.

Your ears clean themselves! You might find earwax gross, but it soaks up loads of dirt and dust, which is then pushed out of the ear by thousands of tiny hairs.

OOOPPPS

A ballet dancer spins really fast but doesn't get dizzy. She has to teach her brain not to think she's still moving once she stops a spin.

Voice and Speech

Speaking and singing—and laughing—are important parts of being human. Robots, too, can communicate. Just don't expect a fun conversation!

Humans learn to speak as children, listening to the people around them and taking in the words for objects, thoughts, and feelings. The brain stores those words and, when needed, sends out a signal when you want to talk. These actions are controlled by a part of the brain called the "Broca's area." Speaking words uses a combination of air and a small organ in the neck called the "larynx," or "voice box."

Air brings oxygen into your body, and without it, you can't speak. When air leaves your lungs, it goes up a thick tube in your neck called the "windpipe." At the top of your neck, the air meets the larynx, which has two thin flaps, called "membranes," that can open and close. The flaps open to let air in and out, and if they push together as air passes, they

The vocal cords open to allow air into the body.

Broca's area—the part of the brain that selects the words you want to speak.

HELLO, BOT

The vocal cords close as air leaves the body. The two membranes vibrate and make a sound. Different vibration speeds make different sounds.

Larynx—where the vocal cords create the sounds for speech.

Air builds in the lungs and passes up the windpipe to the larynx.

vibrate, which makes a sound—your voice! The mouth, tongue, and lips make shapes to turn that sound into a word. Different shapes make different words. When you sing, the same things happen, but more air is pushed through the larynx, and the throat and mouth are "opened" to make a louder sound.

Robots can't copy the complicated speaking system inside a human, but using their computers and other devices, they can speak a limited number of things. They have to be programmed to recognize human voices, especially when those voices ask a bot a question or tell it to do something. A bot "hears" the human voice through a microphone (see pages 60–61). It then uses its computer (its "brain") to figure out the right reply, using sounds stored in its memory. The robot "speaks"

the selection of words through a loudspeaker like the ones in movie theaters. Bots can speak in any language they are programmed to and can sound just like a human. Speaking robots are sometimes called "social robots" and are used in places such as airports and hospitals to give people information when asked. Where else do you think social robots might help people?

TRY THIS...

Your mouth, tongue, and lips change the sounds you make with your voice. Try an A sound. Can you feel your mouth opening up and the sound filling the back of the mouth? Next, make an E sound. Now the sound is at the top of your mouth, which stretches a little. An O sound pulls your cheeks inward, with the noise filling your mouth. Try saying the letters P and B—you have to close your lips tightly and really push the air out!

Microphone—picks up the sounds that the robot's computer recognizes as speech.

HELLO, BOD

Loudspeaker— sends out what the robot's computer thinks is the right reply.

EEEEEEEEEEEEEEEEEEE

Taste and Smell

People would be in big trouble without their sense of taste or smell (food and drink would be so boring). Robots just don't need them.

Taste and smell each do a vital job: taste tells you when you are eating or drinking something that's safe, and smell tells you if something is dangerous to consume. These days, people have a good idea of what is good or bad to eat, but to ancient humans, a good sense of taste and smell kept them alive. Put the two senses together and you get flavor: a signal from the brain that something tastes good—or bad if you are a fussy eater!

When you put something into your mouth, it hits the tongue, which is an organ that's around 3 inches (7.6 cm) long in an adult. The tongue is made mostly of muscle and covered in soft, pink tissue called

"mucosa." It's also covered in about ten thousand taste buds. Each taste bud is topped with tiny hairs that pick up chemicals from foods and drinks mixed with saliva (called "spit"). Taste signals travel into cells—called "taste receptors"— below the tongue's surface and then into nerves that tell the brain what's on your tongue. If it's fresh milk, the brain says, "Yummy!" If it's sour milk, then it says, "Spit it out!"

The sense of smell is really powerful—ten thousand times more powerful than the sense of taste! Smells enter the nasal cavities inside your nose when you breathe. There, they are picked up by little hairs called "cilia," which line the insides of your nose. The cilia send signals to nerve cells called "olfactory receptors," which are joined to nerves called "olfactory nerves." ("Olfactory" is a fancy scientific way of saying "smelling.") The signals travel along these nerves to an area at the top of the nasal cavities, called the "olfactory bulb," and then to the brain, which tells you what you are smelling. Once the data from your nose mixes with the taste data from your tongue, you get the full impact from what you've just consumed—its flavor.

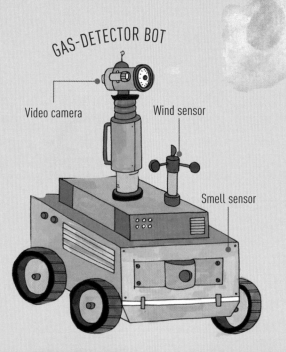

GAS-DETECTOR BOT

Video camera

Wind sensor

Smell sensor

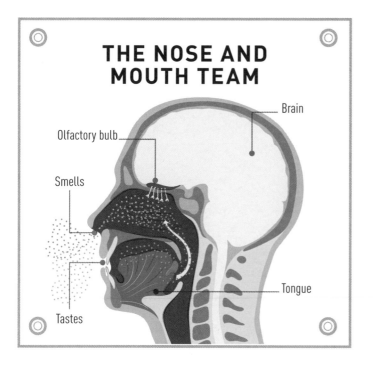

THE NOSE AND MOUTH TEAM

Brain

Olfactory bulb

Smells

Tongue

Tastes

Taste and smell would be wasted on robots. They get their energy from electricity (see pages 42–43), so they don't need food or drink. However, they can be programmed to detect smells and tastes by using sensors to identify chemicals in the air or in substances and collect information about them. These bots can find dangerous substances, such as gases and explosives, and even go into places badly polluted with chemicals that could kill a person. Brave bots!

FANTASTIC FACT

Although you have thousands and thousands of taste buds, there are only five basic kinds of taste:

SWEET Leads you to sugary things—some essential for energy boosts, others not so good for your teeth or weight!

SOUR The sharp, watery-eye taste you find in lemons and vinegar.

BITTER Harmful substances often taste bitter, which stops you from eating them. However, some people like bitter tastes, such as coffee and dark chocolate.

SALTY Sodium (a chemical) makes things such as salt, soy sauce, and olives taste salty. Cooks use salt to improve food's flavor, since it reduces bitterness and brings out sweetness.

UMAMI A rich, meaty taste that you find in mushrooms, ripe tomatoes, and soy sauce (again!). The name comes from the Japanese word for "savoriness."

TASTY!

Robots in Space

Space is one of the most exciting places where robots are used. Unlike humans, they don't need air, food, or water, and they can be sent on missions to places that take years to reach. And they don't need to be brought home again.

Robot probes have been sent to every planet in the solar system and also to some moons. They have even explored comets and asteroids, which fly through space at incredibly fast speeds. Most of these robot space adventures are "flybys," when the robot hurtles past, taking pictures and making measurements with scientific instruments.

Sometimes robots orbit a planet or moon, and sometimes they land on them. Landing is the hardest thing to do, and if it goes wrong, the robot becomes a pile of junk! Because of this risk, it's important that the robot can make its own decisions. For example, it takes between 5 and 20 minutes for a radio signal to travel from Mars to Earth. If a spacecraft landing on Mars sent home a picture showing it was about to crash, there wouldn't be time for a human to tell the spacecraft what to do. So, space robots need to have really advanced computer programming, known as artificial intelligence (see pages 82–83).

FANTASTIC FACTS

- No person has ever set foot on Mars... yet. Maybe you'll be the first to do it!

- Robots have explored the planet. Some robots land and take measurements. Others are rovers that drive around looking for interesting things.

- Rovers have a six-wheel design, so they're very stable. They have a head and neck, with cameras and other instruments, such as spectrometers that test chemicals inside rocks and soil.

- These intelligent robots are—as far as anyone knows—the only life on Mars. It's an actual robot planet!

Space probe Rosetta was the first robot to orbit and land on a comet.

The International Space Station carries six humans around Earth every ninety minutes. Outside it are two powerful robot arms; and a variety of robots reside inside.

Robot probe Cassini made discoveries about Saturn and its moons and rings.

Several robot probes have left the solar system. Voyager 1 was launched in 1977 and is still in contact with Earth.

Sensors on the Curiosity rover measure and record information about Mars's climate and whether there were ever any kind of living things on it.

The Perseverance rover is designed to drill into the surface of Mars to collect samples of rock and soil. It also carries a bot helicopter, called Ingenuity.

CHAPTER 4:
THINKING AND FEELING

Brains of All Kinds

Nearly all animals have brains that tell them what to do. The human brain is big, but it's not the biggest. Robots also need to be told what to do—but their brains are completely different.

The tiniest insect has a brain. The most enormous whale has a brain. You have a brain. It gives you and every creature the instructions to move, eat, drink, sleep, breathe—whatever is needed to stay alive. Some animals are smarter than others and have more complicated brains. The human brain is the most complicated of all because it doesn't just get you to do things. It also tells you to think, keep memories, and have feelings.

Most animals have brains inside their heads. In a human, the brain is close to important things—such as the ears, eyes, nose, and mouth—that control vital senses like

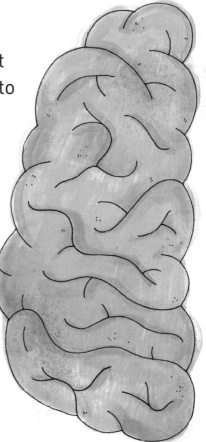

THINK ABOUT THIS...

Humans are the smartest creatures on the planet, so they have the biggest brains, right? Wrong! Big animals often have big brains. A whale, for example, can have a brain four times heavier than a human brain. However, brain size also depends on how many different things an animal has to do. That whale may have a brain that looks big, but it's quite small for such a huge beast. Because humans are so smart, they have a brain that's large compared with their body size. Look at these brains and compare them to the following animals: cat, rat, human, elephant, and chimpanzee. Think of the size and intelligence of each animal and see if you can find its brain.

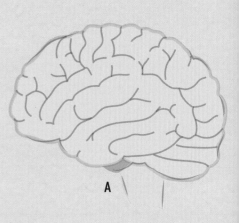

A

sight, hearing, taste, and smell. It means the brain can send signals incredibly quickly to these areas. Your brain is a soft, squishy, gray-pink-white mass that looks like a giant walnut. It's the size of two fists and weighs 2.5 to 3 pounds (1.1 to 1.4 kg). The lumpy folds that cover it allow the brain to cram in many more cells than it could with a smooth surface. The brain is mostly made of fat but also packed with blood vessels and millions of nerve cells called "neurons" (see pages 74–75).

Robots don't need a brain, but they do need something like a brain to process information from their sensors and to make their motors move. For this to happen, a robot needs a computer—or more than one computer—and software programs that contain all the instructions the bot has to follow. In a humanoid robot, its "brain" is sometimes in its head, but it could be anywhere inside—as long as it's protected from damage; a little like the way the human brain is protected by the hard bones of the skull.

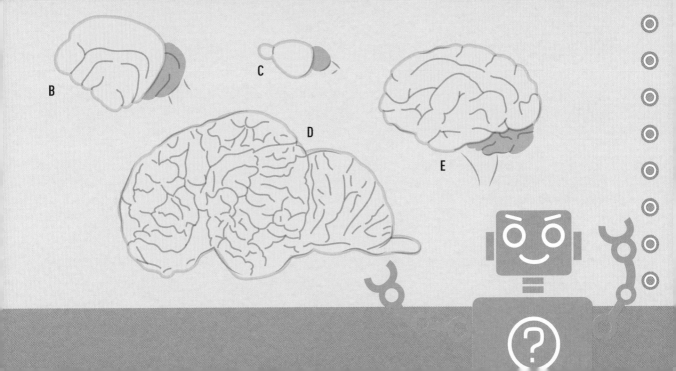

B

C

D

E

How Brains Work

The human brain is one of the wonders of the known universe. No bot comes anywhere near it. Scientists know something about how the brain works, but there's still much to learn.

The brain contains about one hundred billion special nerve cells called "neurons," each one connected to thousands of others (see page 39). That's about the same as the number of stars in the Milky Way. The brain receives tiny electrical signals from the sensory organs—such as eyes, ears, mouth, and fingers—and from around the body, and also sends out instructions. Some instructions are unconscious, meaning we don't realize they're happening ("message to heart: keep pumping").

Just about everything that happens in the body happens because a signal was sent from and to the brain. If you hurt yourself, nerve cells instantly report this to the brain, and you react. You might say "ouch" and rub the area. When you do, the nerve cells send another signal that you have noticed the damage and are trying to fix it. This is sometimes all it takes for the pain to go away.

The largest part of the brain is the cerebrum. Below and at the back of the brain is the cerebellum (sounds similar, looks different). Another part—the brain

Your brain has a left side and a right side. The left side controls all the basic but important stuff, like writing, language, and numbers. The right side gets to control all the fun stuff, like music and art and doing all kinds of creative things.

BRAIN MAP

Different parts of the brain control different actions.

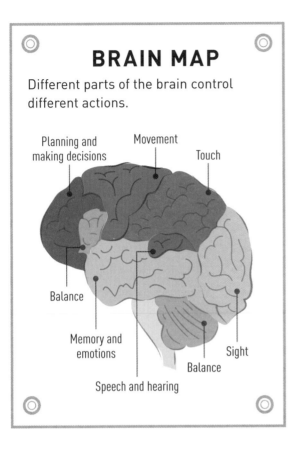

Planning and making decisions

Movement

Touch

Balance

Memory and emotions

Speech and hearing

Balance

Sight

The computer hardware that makes a robot "brain" is like the technology in a laptop or smartphone. The key components are microprocessors. These are little black slabs, each about the size of a postage stamp, with dozens of metal connections, called pins, along the edges. The microprocessors are plugged into circuit boards, which also hold other electronic parts and the wires and cables that connect to the rest of the robot. Some wires connect to the robot's sensors, just like the nerves in a human body. Other wires bring electrical power from batteries, a little like the vessels that carry blood around a human body.

stem—is what joins the brain to the central nervous system running down the spine (see pages 38–39). The cerebrum is divided into left and right halves called "hemispheres." The left half controls the right side of the body, and the right half controls the left of the body. For example, signals from the right eye go to the left half of the brain. The left hemisphere does most of the work for language, writing, math, and hand control. The right hemisphere is linked to creative and artistic ability, as well as imagination. The two halves are about the same size, and both are equally important!

TRY THIS...

What happens when you tickle a friend? They probably laugh—or scream! Now try to tickle yourself. No laughter? When you tickle yourself, your brain is operating your fingers. It knows exactly what's about to happen and warns the body part you are about to touch. This shows how the brain can switch body reactions on and off by changing its signals. Don't bother tickling a bot—you won't get a reaction!

Doctor Bot

Nobody really wants an operation, but millions of people have them each year. There are a lot of operations that need a lot of medics. Calling Dr. Bot!

Surgeons—the doctors who operate on people—have to be really smart and have lots of special skills to work in an operating room. They have to learn about the human body and the things that can go wrong with it. It's important for surgeons to have excellent coordination and be really good with their hands, as well as knowing a lot of medical stuff. The work can be very tiring, and surgeons can't operate when they are not feeling wide-awake. Robots are never tired and can do the same job over and over again for however long it takes. This means robots are good for surgeries and are already being used in hospitals. This will happen more and more in the future.

There are a few kinds of surgical robots. The most advanced have three or four arms—that's at least one more than a surgeon has! These arms might look familiar, since they are very similar to robots used in factories. They can handle tools for cutting and holding, and use all kinds of needles to inject into patients and sew up wounds. They can also take tiny cameras right into the middle of the action and give a close-up view.

FANTASTIC FACT

Some hospitals use cute robot animals, such as baby seals, to help patients recover from surgeries. Furry robot companions reduce stress for patients and the people who care for them.

Computer console

Video screen

SURGEON

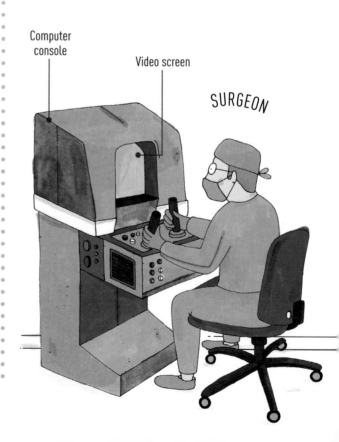

These robots are controlled by human surgeons, who watch what's happening on video screens. What doctors see can be magnified—made bigger—so they know for sure that the bots are making the right moves. Surgeons control the bots' movements with joysticks, like the kinds used for a computer game.

Sometimes the robots only do what the surgeons tell them to do, but other times they are allowed to work on their own. If a patient needs some stitches, called "sutures," the human doctor can tell the robot where these need to go, and the robot can do the tricky sewing by itself. Robot surgery usually means less pain for a patient; a quicker recovery; and smaller, neater scars!

LASER EYES

If you know somebody who has had laser eye surgery, they were probably operated on by a kind of robot. These bots don't have arms like some robots, but they do have very quick reactions. People find it hard to keep their eyes still when a machine is firing a laser at them, and the robot has to make fast adjustments to make up for this.

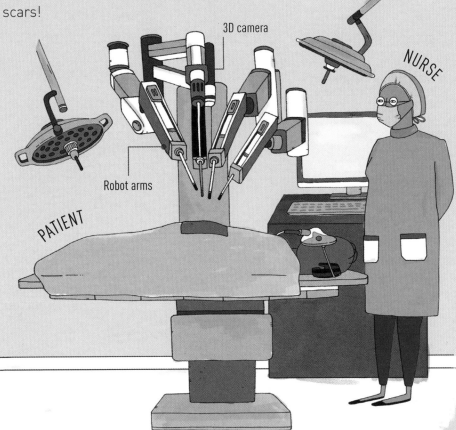

3D camera

Robot arms

PATIENT

NURSE

Mind and Memory

The brain doesn't just send and receive signals. It's also your mind, where information is stored, including all your memories. Sadly, robots don't keep memories like humans do.

You have a physical brain—the gray, squishy organ inside your head—and then there's the brain where the things you feel but can't see are kept. Every experience you have becomes a memory that the brain stores. There are two main types of memory: implicit and explicit. Implicit memories are the really basic ones you use all the time, like how to walk, eat, and react if you touch something hot. Other animals have implicit memories. Explicit memories are the kinds that make you the person you are—friendships, birthday parties, vacations—and that you can share with other people. Explicit memories also include every fact you get from school, books, and the Internet.

Different memories are stored in different parts of the brain, which have some pretty weird names! Implicit memories are handled by the cerebellum and an area called the "basal ganglia," right in the brain's center. Information you don't need to hold on to for long, called "working memories"—like the address of somewhere you need to go—is processed in the prefrontal cortex, at the front of the brain. Explicit memories use three brain parts: the neocortex, hippocampus, and amygdala. The neocortex is the top six layers of the brain and contains data on important stuff like language, movement, and the senses. The hippocampus, in the middle of the brain, looks like a seahorse, which is how it got its name (from the ancient Greek word for a seahorse, *hippokampos*). This area holds memories of events in your life, such as having an ice cream with Grandpa. Sometimes memories move from the hippocampus to the neocortex if they include useful

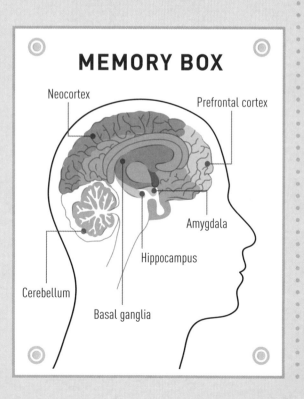

MEMORY BOX

Neocortex

Prefrontal cortex

Amygdala

Hippocampus

Cerebellum

Basal ganglia

information—like "ice cream tastes good."
The almond-shaped amygdala is really
important because it tells you whether
memories are happy or sad.

All these memories make up the story of
your life, which you can dip into and add to
whenever you want. Being able to control
your memories is called "self-awareness."
Robots are not self-aware. Like humans,
they can store loads of information on
their computers about how to do many
complicated things. They can remember
the things they're programmed to do and
to do them better next time. However, a
bot doesn't know if its memories are
happy or sad or how to build memories
into a story about itself. This distinction
makes humans much more interesting
than bots!

THINK ABOUT THIS...
Can you remember what it was like being
a baby? Don't worry, nobody can. Why do
you think that is?

Robots can remember things
if they keep repeating tasks
and are given plenty of
information. A bot might get
to see thousands of photographs
of vegetables, such as eggplant,
carrot, and squash, and be
programmed to know what they
are. If the bot picks up an ear of
corn, and has seen enough photos
of corn, then it knows it's corn!

Getting Emotional

Showing emotion is part of being human, and it's one of the things that makes humans different from other animals. Robots can't feel emotions, but they can copy them.

Everyone has emotions—ones that make you feel good, ones that make you feel bad. According to some psychologists—mind experts—there are six basic emotions: anger, fear, surprise, disgust, joy, and sadness. All other emotions come from these six. If you have a pet, you will know that an animal can have feelings, but no animal can feel as many emotions as a human.

Fear is a very powerful emotion that helps humans survive. If a person is in danger and feels fear, it triggers something called the "fight-or-flight response." The heart starts pounding, and breathing gets heavy. This prepares the person to either stand and face the danger or run away to escape. Pain also sparks emotions, which help the body to react in a way that will tackle the cause of the pain.

All emotions are controlled by the limbic system, which is buried deep inside the brain. The most important parts of this system are the hippocampus and the amygdala (see pages 78–79). The hippocampus holds memories, while the amygdala adds emotions, such as pleasure or anxiety, to those memories. A memory with an attached emotion is much more likely to stay in the brain.

ANGER   JOY   SURPRISE   DISGUST

The amygdala also causes an emotion when things happen to you, like happiness from getting a present or disgust from smelling something bad.

Robots don't react to pain or fear—in fact, they have no emotions at all. However, some humanoid bots can be programmed to react to emotions in the same way as humans. Their computers activate motors that move parts of the face into a smile, scowl, or other expression. Also, the voice programmed into a bot's computer (see pages 64–65) can include styles of speech that show emotion, such as laughter and anger. In 1998, the first robot to show facial expressions was developed. Named Kismet, it had sixteen computers and a mouth, eyes, and ears. It was programmed to react to the faces of people it saw through its cameras and had a small vocabulary. If someone smiled at Kismet, it smiled back! Kismet could also look angry, sad, and surprised.

In 2016, engineers turned on a robot named Sophia, which has a real-looking human face that can show more than sixty different reactions. Sophia responds to the things it sees and can also have simple conversations with people. It can tell jokes, and Sophia was even on a late-night talk show!

THINK ABOUT THIS...

Some emotions make you have a strong reaction. Why do you think people cry when something painful or sad happens?

SADNESS

FEAR

WHAT'S UP WITH THEM?

The computer inside a robot can tell the robot what emotion a human is showing. But a bot wouldn't be able to understand the emotion. That's a little sad!

Who's the Smartest?

Humans are smart in all kinds of ways. They are smart enough to build robots that do amazing things. But can a robot ever be as smart as you?

Smartness is often called "intelligence," but there's more than one type of intelligence. Some people are good at math and science. Others are good at poetry and writing or at painting and drawing. Everyone is good at different things, which makes life more interesting for all people.

Being good at different things is possible because of the billions of neurons in the brain. They work together to produce action and movement but also to build memories and ideas and process lots of information. Each neuron (see page 39)

creates thousands of new connections with other neurons, and they constantly grow as they solve new problems. All you have to do to grow these connections is to use your brain to think about things. It's just like exercising your arms or legs—doing brain exercises makes the brain stronger.

A robot has connections, like the one between its computer and sensors, but these are a fixed number and can't grow like the neurons in your brain. This means a bot's intelligence is limited by the power of its computer. Scientists and engineers

Computer programs have beaten the world's best chess players, but this doesn't mean they are truly intelligent.

are working to create robots that can do all the things humans can do—such as stand or walk—but also make their own decisions—like when to stand or walk. This is called "artificial intelligence," or "AI."

Some computers can beat the best humans at complicated strategy games like chess. Automobiles that drive themselves seem pretty smart (see pages 50–51). However, these machines are not self-aware like humans (see pages 78–79) and do only what they have been programmed to do. You could ask a robot, "Hey, robot, do you know who you are," and it might say yes. But it could just be programmed to say that!

Robots contain thousands of tiny devices called "transistors," which allow electricity to flow through them, connecting all the different working parts. Today, there are powerful supercomputers that have more transistors than a human brain has neurons. But they still can't create new connections like your brain can—and they're huge! Maybe in the future one of these machines will become self-aware and think for itself, but that is still a long way off.

TRY THIS...

One way to work out whether a robot really is intelligent is with the Turing test (named for a famous mathematician): if a person can't tell they are having an online chat with a human or a machine, the robot has passed the test. You can do your own Turing test using the virtual assistant on a smartphone or a smart speaker. Ask it how it's feeling or which football team it supports. The answers can be really funny. You may quickly learn two things: these devices can be really useful, but they are certainly not self-aware.

Bot Explorers

Humans are great explorers, but some places are too dangerous or difficult for them to get to. Time to send in the robots!

The human body is pretty tough—tough enough for explorers to climb the highest mountains, cut their way through the thickest jungles, or cross the hottest deserts. However, the body can't survive too much heat or cold or too much pressure—like at the bottom of the deepest seas. Humans are also limited to where they can explore by their size. You try squeezing through a gap that's only a few inches wide!

DEEP-SEA BOTS Robot diving machines can reach the deepest parts of the ocean— almost 7 miles (11.3 km) down. They can be controlled from the surface by an expert diver. Some bot divers even look like human divers!

Because robots are made of tough and strong metals, plastics, and rubber, they can work in extreme places where a softer human body couldn't. If a person dived too deep into the sea, they would pass out and get very sick. Robot divers can carry on exploring no matter how deep they go. The lava inside a volcano can reach a temperature of more than 2,000 degrees Fahrenheit (1,090 degrees Celsius). If humans went anywhere close to that, they would be fried! Special volcano bots on wheels can get near lava and record lots of useful information for volcano scientists (called "volcanologists"). Robots can also work longer, harder, and more safely than

VOLCANO BOTS Small but highly mobile robots can explore openings in a volcano—called "vents"—where the hot lava escapes. They can take samples of rocks, chemicals, and gases.

humans in difficult conditions. Under the ground, there are many important substances, like iron and copper, that people need to make things like cars. These materials have to be dug out, which can be dangerous work. Robot diggers and drillers can do the work nonstop, and they are controlled at a safe distance by human operators.

ANCIENT DISCOVERIES

Some ruins from long ago, especially the tombs of kings and queens, are unexplored because a person can't get in without using explosives and causing great damage. (Tombs are places where people used to bury their dead.) Archaeologists—scientists who study these kinds of sites—have created robots that can fit through very small gaps in the walls of ancient tombs. The scientists drill holes in the wall and push the specially built robot through the gap to reach the inside of the tomb. Then they can control the robot by computer as it films what it sees.

MINING BOTS Computer-controlled robots can dig and drill much farther and deeper than a human miner. Most importantly, they keep people out of harm's way.

Bodiless Bots

Some bots are invisible! Even though you can't see them, they are all around you, doing good things and not-so-good things.

Young or old, short or tall, girl or boy, everyone has to live inside a body. Being invisible is something people can only dream about. Robots are usually solid things, in all shapes and sizes, but there are bots that have no physical form and live inside machines. They can repeat simple tasks over and over again—way faster than any human. One of these bots is called a "virtual assistant," which is a voice inside a device that listens to your questions and gives answers. It also does what you ask it to, like "play me some happy music." When you ask the virtual assistant a question, it's picked up by a microphone on the machine, turned into digital information, and sent to a big collection of computers that search the Internet for the answer. The information is sent back to the "assistant," and it "tells" you the answer.

SPIDERS!

CHATBOXES!

CRAWLERS!

GOOD BOTS, BAD BOTS

How about invisible creepy-crawlies? Inside the Internet, there are bots that search for and pick up information and send messages. They are called "spiders" or "crawlers." Each is a little piece of software that wanders around the Internet, gathering data from websites. These are useful bots—without them, you wouldn't be able to find all that interesting stuff online and find it so quickly. But some of these bots are "bad" bots that can "infect" a computer like a disease. Criminals do this so they can steal information, and even money, from people.

These days, people do more and more things on computers and smartphones, like shopping or checking their money. This means that people are not talking face-to-face with a person. Instead, they have to work with a machine. There are bots, called "chatbots," that can copy the kinds of conversation you might have with a person working in a shop or bank. A chatbot studies a new message and, using computer software, figures out what the person wants to do, such as, "I want to put fifty dollars into my bank account." It then sends one or more messages back, telling the person that what they wanted has been done. Chatbots help people feel like they are talking to a real person rather than a robot!

FANTASTIC FACT

Where would you be without the Internet! It's so important for finding out loads of vital and interesting things. However, it can be used by criminals to steal from people, often by spreading a bot called a "virus" through the Internet and into computers. This is called "cybercrime." In 2004, criminals used a virus called "MyDoom" to get into people's computers through e-mails. It was the most expensive virus ever. People lost $38.5 billion!

Bots and Us—the Future

Scientists and engineers are making smarter and smarter robots. In the future, bots will be able to do many things. But could they get too smart?

Humans need their bodies. Muscles, bones, organs, and especially the brain allow you to do amazing things—including stuff that robots will probably never be able to do. However, people will always be more easily damaged than robots—and they will get older. Many bots already help people, making their lives easier and safer—and there will be more friendly and supportive robots as time goes by.

THINK ABOUT THIS...

Some people don't like the idea of robots doing everything for humans. In the 1940s, Isaac Asimov, a science-fiction author, wrote the Three Laws of Robotics. These laws said that robots could not let a human be hurt; they had to obey orders from humans; and they should not let themselves be hurt. What do you think would happen if robots became as smart, or smarter, than humans? And when do you think that might happen?

In hospitals, robots will do even more operations. Surgeons will be able to replace damaged organs such as hearts or lungs with robotic organs, allowing people to live better and longer lives. Tiny bots will be injected into bodies to attack tumors in cancer patients, and larger bots will take samples from inside bodies, with hardly a mark left on the person! For people recovering from operations, carebots will help look after them and keep them happy.

There will be more robots in the home. Scientists are working on robots that will be more like humans, with arms, hands, and fingers that can pick things up, clean rooms, cook meals, and even pour you a drink. And nobody likes cleaning the bathroom! Robots will soon be there, too, making sure everything is sparkling clean and ready to do even the dirtiest jobs.

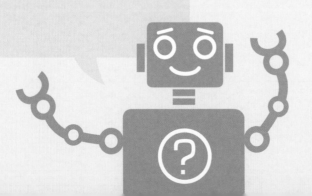

Robot buses and smart cars are already a reality (see pages 50–51). In the future, robot planes could fly with no pilot at the controls. It would save money, but some people may be too nervous to fly with no one in the cockpit! Robots will continue to explore space, with bot spacecraft making more and more trips to Mars to prepare the planet as a place where humans could live. Many robot-controlled objects (satellites) orbit, or circle, Earth, taking photos, checking the weather, and bouncing signals around so people can use GPS and other communications systems. These satellites have to be launched from Earth, but in the future, they could be built in space by special bots using 3D printers and materials launched from the planet.

WE'RE A GREAT TEAM!

Answers

CHAPTER 1: BODY BASICS
PAGE 13:

Red kangaroo, forty days; Indian elephant, up to twenty-two months (the longest of any mammal); white-eared opossum, twelve days (the shortest of any mammal); horse, up to twelve months; chimpanzee, about eight months; robots—any time from an hour to years and years!

PAGE 19:

There are seven degrees of freedom in your arm, not counting the hand: in the shoulder (3—up and down, forward and backward, side to side), the elbow (1—up and down), and the wrist (3—up and down, side to side, rotation).

PAGE 24:

The Achilles tendon sits at the back of the foot and joins your calf muscle (the lowest muscle in your leg) to your heel bone (the bottom part of your foot on the opposite end from your toes). It has to be very strong, since it's this tendon that provides the spring that lifts your foot when you run or jump. Achilles was one of the greatest warriors in ancient Greek mythology, and he fought in the Trojan War. The only place where he could be wounded was just above his heel—the Achilles tendon.

CHAPTER 2: GET MOVING
PAGE 46:

When the first female humans walked, their bodies had to adapt. Their pelvises—the bones between the tummy and the hips—changed shape, and the openings that babies passed through before they were born got narrower. For babies to fit through the narrower openings, they had to have smaller heads, which meant that their brains had to do most of their development after the babies were born! After around a year, babies' brains have developed enough to allow them to take their first steps.

PAGE 49:

Gazelles have more slow-twitch muscles. Cheetahs have mostly fast-twitch muscles.

CHAPTER 3: SEEING AND SENSING
PAGE 57:

The human eye has many more pixels than a smartphone camera—around 576 million pixels (576 megapixels)!

PAGE 58:

When you turn off the robot alarm clock, it lets you snooze for a while. But then it rolls and jumps off the bedside table and dashes around the bedroom on its two little wheels. To turn off the alarm, you have to chase and catch the bot. Now, you are up and wide awake!

PAGE 61:

Breathing .... 10 decibels
Refrigerator .... 40 decibels
Regular rainfall........... 50 decibels
Alarm clock................. 80 decibels
City traffic................... 85 decibels
Hippopotamus .... 114 decibels
Jet plane taking off..... 140 decibels
Firecrackers .... 160 decibels

CHAPTER 4: THINKING AND FEELING
PAGE 72:

A = human
B = cat
C = rat
D = elephant
E = chimpanzee

PAGE 79:

Scientists are still trying to figure out why we can't remember what it was like to be babies, but it could have something to do with brain size and information overload. When a baby is born, their brain is only one-quarter the size of an adult brain. By the time a child is two years old, their brain has reached three-quarters its full size. Babies have to absorb lots of information so they can develop quickly. This means there isn't much room for explicit memories to be kept.

PAGE 81:

When you feel pain or sadness, your body's reaction is to get rid of the bad feelings. Your tears, which are released through crying, contain hormones and endorphins that help you feel better.

PAGE 89:

Robots are getting smarter and smarter, but humans still make and control them. In 2016, researchers at the University of Oxford, in England, and Yale University, in the United States, asked around 350 science and industry experts to say when robots might get smarter than humans. They thought that by 2060 robots could probably do pretty much anything a human could do. Then they would completely overtake humans by 2136. What happens after that is guesswork. Humans would still need bots, but bots might not need bods anymore!

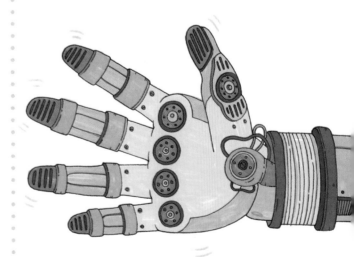

Index

Picture Credits

All illustrations were produced by
Tilly (www.runningforcrayons.co.uk),
except for the following: